Finding
HEALING
FROM THE ANGUISH OF
Favoritism

JAMES OFFUTT

Finding
HEALING
FROM THE ANGUISH OF
Favoritism

In the Home, Church, and Workplace

SEL PUBLICATIONS
Syracuse, New York

Finding Healing From the Anguish of Favoritism
Copyright © 2014 by James Offutt

ISBN 978-1-93725-32-7

Published by:
Sel Publications
Syracuse, NY

I would like to dedicate this book to my Lord and Savior Jesus Christ who directed me to write this book. Also, to all the men and women of Teen Challenge plus the other children, men, and women who's poignant stories stirred me when writing this book.

I pray that every reader will find hope and help from the ravages of favoritism in their lives.

Acknowledgements

I would like to acknowledge my wife, Connie, for her ideas and help in reading and correcting my manuscript.

To my fine editor, Tim Bennett, for his insightful corrections and helpful ideas including my title.

In addition, to my friends Rick and Hank for their encouragement and support.

Contents

Introduction

My first two books, *Anger Reconciliation* and *From Bitterness to Reconciliation*, focused on the problems people have with expressing anger, handling conflict, and overcoming bitterness. In each case, I felt God leading me to write about that particular subject, and the same is true of favoritism. Each subject had, or does have, a significant role in affecting many people's lives, usually in a destructive manner. Upon selecting favoritism as my topic, I began searching for books on favoritism and found none in the library with only a couple on Amazon. There were no Christian books written entirely on the subject. In fact, there were very few books at all written on the subject.

Most of the books have been authored by secular psychologists or writers that have experienced partiality in their lives. They discuss favoritism as a child, sibling, or adult within the family. These books exclude the larger aspects of favoritism that I discuss such as favoritism in the church and the workplace. As far as I can determine, this book will be the first Christian book to cover favoritism entirely in all these different areas. While it starts in the family, we all encounter it in some form or another in each stage of our lives. Thus, this book will devote separate chapters on favoritism in our family (chapters 1-4, 6 &7), in the Bible (chapter 8), in the church. (chapter 9), workplace (chapter 10), and God's favor in our lives (chapter 12).

We all feel the effects of some form favoritism at sometime in our lives, either as a favored one, unfavored one, or an overlooked one. Often the favored one learns how to maintain their status through the different stages of their life. However, it is possible to be the favorite one in the family now, but have that change as we move through life. Unfortunately, if the favored one continues to demonstrate the downside characteristics of favoritism in their lives, then those around him will find their lives are negatively affected by this behavior. I wrote this book to help each of the three types (favored, unfavored, and overlooked) to find help from God and solace with their particular status. Each of the three categories mentioned above have their advantages and disadvantages, which I will discuss in detail. The real problem is that intentional (dysfunctional) favoritism divides families, churches, and workplaces. Favoritism is a sin against God's commandment because He wants us to treat everyone equally with love and without partiality.

In my research, I found there were few books that discussed the three different types in detail and none from a Christian perspective. In collecting material for the book, I interviewed people, Teen Challenge students, adults, parents, employees, and pastors on their personal experiences with favoritism. Also, I learned about their personal experience as a: favorite one, unfavored one, or overlooked one. I was struck by the anguish expressed by their many compelling stories from being favored or unfavored by their parents, pastors, or bosses. Their poignant stories are included in this book with their names changed. In addition, I have included stories from my own life that help illustrate when I was a favorite, unfavored, or an overlooked one as I experienced it at one time or another in my life. It is my hope that these stories will help you comprehend the personal devastation that intentional favoritism has inflicted on individuals, families, and society.

While some people have attempted to address this problem, most overlook it or deny it, hoping it will go away. Its vestiges, however, can linger in the victim's mind creating adults with ongoing bitterness toward their parents, siblings, pastors, and employers. I found brothers and sisters that haven't talked to each other for years, families divided, and churches split because of favoritism's effects. With such lasting destruction going on, I believe that it is essential that this topic be discussed and addressed more frequently for the emotional and spiritual health of everyone.

As a Christian, I am seeking in this book to help all people, especially Christians, to become aware of it, address it, and utilize the Christian principles put forth in this book to stop its devastation. My goal is to bring true healing and hope to those suffering from the pain that favoritism can bring. I feel that the Christian approach to healing the negative partiality we've experienced in our lives will provide us with the most effective approach to complete healing. We know that God wants to heal us completely from the resentment of favoritism and, thereby, help us to start new lives free of its damaging effects.

— *Jim Offutt*

Chapter 1
What is Favoritism?

"Favoritism destroyed my life!" exclaimed David, a man in his late 40s, in a voice filled with pain. His father left the family when David was four. David went on to tell me how his grandparents had almost entirely raised him from a toddler until he was 17. His grandmother, Joann, particularly loved him with words of encouragement and tender hugs. She favored him over his younger brother Phil, who preferred to stay at home with their mother, Edna, who favored him. Phil almost never came over to Joann's house although it was within easy walking distance from their parent's home. After school, David would go right over to Joann's house and stay there until after dinner. Soon the bond between the child and the grandmother had become equivalent to that of mother and child.

As time went on, Edna's constant partiality of Phil drove David even closer to his grandmother. In effect, the two brothers' main relationships were dominated by favoritism. As a result, their interrelationship became plagued with fierce competition at home, school, and into adulthood. Edna continues to favor Phil to this very day while David feels sadly estranged from his mother. Instead, David seeks solace from dear friends outside the family. David doesn't speak or communicate with his brother and only infrequently with his mother. "My family is fractured by favoritism even now," David responded despondently. "Favoritism is deadly. If I could change anything, I wish I had never been favored. Being favored always makes things worse."

From this life story, we see the painful effects of favoritism on the siblings and the whole family. Not only are the main participants affected, but their families and friends are swept into partiality's devastation as well. Soon enemy camps are formed that sadly won't relate with each other unless absolutely necessary. The unhappy effect of such abusive favoritism can last for years and even generations unless someone breaks it. Ironically, the originators will say they were just trying to love someone they liked or with whom they share a similar personality. The situation, however, becomes a problem when the parent(s) focuses most of their care on one child to the exclusion of the other child leaving a lasting memory of anger and pain in the unfavored, or overlooked child.

Favoritism begins with the parents innate survival needs to insure that their family name and values live on after their deaths. Consequently, parents tend to favor the strongest, prettiest, and healthiest child as they will be able to continue the family line. While each parent has preferences, they usually try not to show it to their children. Nevertheless, we will all encounter favoritism in any of our relationships either in the family, workplace, or church. No one is really immune from its effects either as a favored one, the unfavored one, or the overlooked one. Favoritism abusively impacts us when a person in authority frequently denies us love, attention, and/or opportunities for no just reason. Such partiality, in time, creates a deep resentment that ruptures our relationship with the authority person, often someone close to us. In this book, I intend to explore favoritism in all these areas of our lives: family, church, and workplace. I will also use examples from the Bible when discussing favoritism from a Christian perspective. James 2:1 commands us, as Christians, to not engage in favoritism: "*My brothers, as believers in our glorious Jesus Christ, don't show favoritism.*" (Note all Bible verses are from the NIV Bible).This verse is easy to say but much harder to accomplish, but it is possible with God's help.

A definition of favoritism is the practice of giving consistently preferred treatment to one child, or member, or employee, over the treatment of others in the group. As a result, the favored one continually follows the wishes of the authority to continue to get special treatment. The equation for favoritism is:

An authority figure is strongly attracted to one child, employee, or member → the authority wants to make them feel special over their competitors → The authority gives him/her gifts, promotions, and praise while excluding equally qualified others → the favored one follows the direction of the authority and develops strong self-confidence but also a feeling of entitlement → the favored one breaks boundaries and fails to develop close relationships → develops a prideful attitude → walks away from God and His principles → the favored one reaps the anguish of such actions and attitude.

This equation is the cycle of favoritism from "the favored one's" point of view. It reflects the fact that the favored one didn't ask to be favored although all children, members, and employees strive to be liked by their authority figure(s). In the equation, we see how being a favored one builds self-esteem and confidence, which often enables him/her to achieve great worldly success. Such achievement becomes an elixir to the favorite causing them to strive harder resulting in them attaining high positions. At the same time, they can easily develop destructive behaviors such as: the sense that they are entitled to the best positions, rewards, and benefits without the same hard work that others must endure for the same reward. Also, their self-centered attitude causes the favored one to dismiss any need for a connection with God, instead they look to themselves and their favoring authority.

If this sense of entitlement is not constrained by God or someone else, the "favored one" feels he can do anything he/she pleases without negative consequences. Their sinful nature starts to control his/her thinking and desires. Such an attitude is ripe for breaking boundaries including the law. When such actions occur, the "favored one" pays a heavy price such as jail, shame, or public humiliation. Also, the people closest to the "favored one" may incur the heavy price of destructive favoritism even though they may have been innocent from starting it.

The "favored one" struggles to develop peer relationships as they are not accustomed to the give-and-take of such associations. They have built up such a prideful attitude by getting what they want, which sabotages their personal relationships. Most people want a sharing relationship so favored ones often end up living a lonely existence. They fail to understand why everyone doesn't like them, or want to be with them. These are some of the advantages and disadvantages of favoritism in one's life. I'll go into greater detail in chapter three. Let us keep in mind that God considers favoritism as sinful and every person as special to Him.

Often parents claim that they treat each child the same in order to avoid any appearance of favoritism. In reality, such an approach fails to acknowledge or work effectively with different abilities, personalities, and interests unique to each child. A child with disabilities may require more parental attention as shown by the following true story:

> When I went to school for the first grade, I had to read aloud to the class. When I tried to read the sentence, I always mixed up the words and the other kids would always laugh at me. I felt so embarrassed and ashamed. Soon, I just hated going to school and my confidence crashed. Was I just stupid? My mother, to her credit, told me "No, you are not stupid. With persistence, I will help you overcome this handicap. Just never give up trying." The illness I had is now called dyslexia. She would spend long hours helping me to read correctly. I learned to slow down and let my mind correctly organize the words.
>
> When my sister, two years younger, saw all this attention I was getting she asked if she could also learn to read. Obviously, she also wanted my mother's attention. Consequently, my mother would often have us both working on reading, but my sister learned faster since she didn't have my problem. Gradually with consistent effort, God's help, and my mother's, I was able to read correctly and today I have no problem

reading. I will always be thankful for my mother's help and her wise words to "Never give up." Learning this valuable lesson on perseverance, I have been able to overcome many obstacles in my life. I am very grateful to her efforts.

As a first son, however, my mother did favor me. Somehow I appealed to her as she told me "You are such a good looking baby." I did nothing of my own accord to warrant her attention, I just got it. Such is the beginning of favoritism. Ellen Webber Libby PhD in her book, *The Favorite Child,* confirms this: "Generally, sons growing up as the unquestioned favorite of one parent are likely to achieve great professional success."

The concept of equal treatment, or fairness, for all children really doesn't work for the parents, or the children. Each child has different needs so meeting each child's needs is more effective for everyone than equal treatment for every child. One parent, when pressed by her children about her unequal treatment, exclaimed "I try to spread my unfairness around equally." A thoughtful targeted approach towards each child helps that child grow to their greatest potential. Just as a very intelligent child could go to a demanding college, such a school might result in an average child failing. Consequently, equality for every person does not meet their needs and could easily become destructive to them.

HOW DOES FAVORITISM DEVELOP

Selecting a favorite friend, or meal, is a normal part of life for us. With people, we naturally gravitate toward those with similar personalities, interests or values. We just seem to understand each other and get along better with those who react and think like we do. Thus, we enjoy a comfort from being and talking with that person.

While, we as an authority figure might favor a child, worker, or member over others, we might impose our aspirations on that person ignoring their expectations and abilities. However, if we believe that our personal needs are linked closely to their achievement, we are on the dangerous path toward dysfunctional favoritism. In this case, we will pour most of our resources and attention, over an extended time, into the success of the "favored one" to the exclusion of the qualified others. The "favored one" often becomes disliked by the unfavored and overlooked ones. A special bond develops between the authority and the favored one whereby the authority will manipulate the actions and beliefs of the favored one to reach the goals of the authority person. Bonnie Angelos highlights this situation in her book, *First Mothers: the Women Who Shaped the Presidents*. She describes how the mothers of all the presidents from 1932 to 2008 favored their sons to exclusion of their other children and manipulated them for great political success to become presidents.

Regrettably, a family history of favoritism will often infect succeeding generations. The actions of a favoring parent are unconsciously imprinted on the brain of the favored child, who then feels compelled to replicate the same on one of their children. Exodus 34:7 speaks of the dangers of such a generational curse: *"The Lord . . . does not leave the guilty unpunished; he punishes the children and their children for the sin of their fathers to the third and fourth generation."*

Consequently, it is important, as Christians, to avoid showing dysfunctional favoritism to our children, employees, or members. Jesus, while on earth, treated each person differently and kindly. He realized he needed to rebuke Peter, the impetuous apostle, several times. One example is Luke 22:33-34: *"But he (Peter) replied 'Lord, I am ready to go with you to prison and to death.' Jesus answered, 'I tell you, Peter, before the rooster crows today, you will deny me three times that you know me.'"* Yet, Jesus was more compassionate with Thomas's disbelief in His resurrection in John 20 24-28: *"Now Thomas (called Didymus), one of the Twelve was not with the disciples when Jesus came. So the other disciples told him, 'We have seen the Lord!'*

But he said to them, 'Unless I see the nail marks in his hands and put my finger where the nails were, and put my hand into his side, I will not believe it.'

A week later . . . Thomas was with them. Though the doors were locked, Jesus came and stood among then and said . . . to Thomas 'Put your finger here; see my hands. Reach out your hand and put it into my side. Stop doubting and believe.'

Thomas said to him, 'My Lord and my God!'"

Some other characteristics of favoritism in the family some of which are from Ellen Libby Webber's book, *The Favorite Child* (marked with an *) are:

*1. Favoritism is not inherently good or bad, but on how the parents listen to their children's complaints about it. Are they receptive to try to understand the truth of the situation? The children know which one of them has been favored.

2. The quality of the communications, understanding or defensive, between the parents sets the atmosphere for favoritism in the family. Do the parents work together to deal effectively with any abusive favoritism?

3. Families that are open and honest with each other can prevent abusive favoritism from getting started. Such approaches by the parents model the same behavior in their children.

*4. The dynamics of favoritism exist in both small and large families.

Summary:

1. Favoritism begins with the parent's desire to continue the family line—tend to favor the strongest, prettiest, and healthiest children. We find favoritism in the family, workplace, and church. No one is immune.

3. When an authority denies us love, attention and/or opportunities for no just reason, we feel the pain of abusive favoritism. This hurt can cause us to break our relationship with the authority person(s). James 2:1.

4. The equation for favoritism is: **An authority figure is strongly**

attracted to a dependent → the authority wants them to feel special by giving them gifts, promotions, and praise → The favored one follows the direction of the authority and develops strong self-confidence but also a sense of entitlement → favored one breaks boundaries and fails to develop close relationships → develops a prideful attitude → walks away for God and His principles → reaps the anguish of such actions.

5. Equal treatment (fairness) for children doesn't work for parents or children. It fails to meet the different needs of each child.

6. Sources of favoritism:

a. Selecting a favorite friend or meal is natural.

b. Favoritism is dysfunctional when an authority figure's needs are linked to the achievement of the favored one. The authority puts resources, and attention toward the "favored one" to help them reach the authority figure's goals.

c. Generational favoritism is a curse. A parent imprints their actions on the brain of the favored child, who repeats it with their children. Exodus 34:7. God's people are commanded to avoid dysfunctional favoritism. Jesus treated each person differently—rebuking Peter (Luke 22:33-34) vs. compassion for Thomas (John 20: 24-28).

d. Characteristics of favoritism from Ellen Libby Webber's book, *The Favorite Child* (marked by an *) are:

*1). Favoritism is not good or bad, but on how parents listen to their children's complaints. Children know if one of them has been favored.

2). The interactions, understanding or defensive, between the parents sets the atmosphere for favoritism.

3). Families that are honest with each other can prevent abusive favoritism.

*4). The dynamics of favoritism exist in small or large families.

Discussion Questions

1. What is favoritism? What is dysfunctional favoritism?

2. What was your experience with favoritism in your family? If so, were you the favorite, unfavored, or overlooked one?

   What was your experience with favoritism in the workplace?

   What was your experience with favoritism in the church?

3. What is the problem with equal treatment for each child?

   Did you experience this?

   If so, did it work for you?

4. Name two characteristics of favoritism?

Chapter 2
How Favoritism Originates in the Home, Church, and Workplace

Research by Jill Soitor, research sociologist, has shown several reasons for favoritism in the family to include:

Parents are drawn to a child's behavior and/or personality that more closely resembles their own. This allows them to usually connect emotionally much easier. Likewise, children with opposite personalities incur much greater discipline and discouraging words. There are some exceptions where similar personalities clash. As girls tend to be more compliant, they tend to be favored more frequently. According to Jacqueline Plumez, a psychologist, who studied adopted children found, "what matters most is whether your temperaments are simpatico."

Parents under increased stress tend to more easily demonstrate their favoritism to a particular child. Often, they will select the one they think that will be most capable of success in the world.

Often the first-born or last-born is picked as the favorite. Meanwhile middle children have little chance of being selected as they always have another sibling(s) to compete with for the favored position. Generally last-born is the most loved, while the first-born gets most of the privileges.

If the child has the same gender as the parent, often there is a greater kinship with that child. Their interests and thoughts are frequently quite similar, which draws them together. In some cultures, particularly Spanish and Asian, boys are favored first by both genders. In Chinese families girls are the ones most frequently aborted. If there is only one child of a gender out of several in the family, then that child will often become the favored one.

Sources of favoritism in the workplace or church include:

You have a similar personality as the pastor or manager or other church leader.

You are a compliant, hard worker who doesn't challenge the authority.

You are of the same race, ethnic background or hold the same religion as the authority.

DIFFERENT TYPES OF INTENTIONAL FAVORITISM IN THE FAMILY, SCHOOL, OR CHURCH

There are several different types of intentional favoritism by the authority in the family, church, or workplace. Such partiality is shown consciously by an authority in the following ways:

Preferential favoritism by providing greater opportunities to learn or advance to a certain child, employee, or member compared to the other equally qualified person. This form of discrimination breeds resentment in the unfavored others, which can lead to morale problems in the group.

Drawing comparisons between children, members, or employees as a means of motivation usually has the opposite effect. The less favored one feels rejected causing greater anger by such an action. When these comparisons are made, they overlook the other strong qualities of the person (we discuss this topic in greater detail in chapter 6). The authority is in fact making a dangerous value judgment of what they think is better.

I can remember my father telling me, "Why can't you spell like your sister?" As a slow learner, I struggled to keep up academically with my younger sister, who seemed to thrive in school. I would feel so inadequate academically. The comparison hurt as spelling and grammar seemed so foreign to me. I just couldn't seem to grasp them. The feeling of being less than my sister hovered over me for several years. My confidence in myself and my abilities faltered.

Then I went into history class in fifth grade. There, my strong memory helped me to excel. I would get "As" on every test and the teacher would publicly acknowledge me. Then, my self-confidence soared. I loved history so much that I would come home from school and read it for enjoyment. It was then that my father finally recognized that I had intelligence.

Discriminatory favoritism involves giving rewards, freedoms, and resources to a favored one over an equally qualified one. Such inequity leads to frustration and rage in the unfavored one and can rupture any friendship that may have existed between them.

Prejudicial favoritism is the unjust expression by an authority by using compliments, or attention given extensively to someone to the exclusion of someone else. This blatant partiality creates hostile feelings in the less favored one.

These forms of intentional favoritism arise from an authority's strong desire to use a favored one to achieve their own goals. While there are some slight forms of favoritism in every organization, it is when this favoritism is accentuated that serious problems develop. In fact, when such favoritism becomes rampant in the group—be it a family, church or company—this behavior may be delay or even defeat the group's goals. I will be discussing ways to overcoming intentional favoritism in the subsequent chapters.

As children we are not able to select our birth order, gender, physical appearance or personalities. Consequently, we have little control over who is selected as the favorite. It is the parent(s) who make that decision to gratify their needs. Favoritism, especially intentional favoritism, is against God's law of unconditional love to: *"love your neighbor as yourself."* The Apostle Paul opposes favoritism in 1 Timothy 5:21, where he admonishes us: *"I charge you, in the sight of God and Christ Jesus and the elect angels, to keep these instructions without partiality, and to do nothing out of favoritism.*" We live in a society that seeks to make favorites out of the rich, beautiful, talented, or bright. Instead, God wants us to honor those whose heart is like Christ—loving everyone without exception.

As children in the family, you are all either selected to be the favored one, unfavored one, or overlooked one. Our parents choose which one you are going to be without considering your desires. Each type is discussed in detail in the following two chapters so as to help you identify which one you are. Remember, you may start out being the favorite and later become the unfavored in the family so your position depends on the desires and expectations of your parents. The true danger is when your parent(s) are so intense in their favoritism of one child that they exclude the other children. We call this dysfunctional or intentional favoritism.

Summary:

1. Jill Soitor, sociologist, reasons for family favoritism include: Both parent and child have the same personality. Parents under stress select the most successful child. Often the first-born or last-born are favorites. The last-born is the most loved while the first–born gets the privileges.

The child of the same gender as the parent is favored. In some cultures, boys are favored by both genders. The only one child of one gender is usually favored.

2. Sources of favoritism in the school or church include: A similar personality as the boss, pastor, or church leader. A compliant, hard worker who doesn't challenge the authority. The same race, ethnic background, or religion as the authority.

3. Different types of intentional favoritism are when an authority shows the following:

a. Preferential favoritism—providing greater opportunities to one person to learn.

b. Making comparisons—between children, or members is a means of motivation leads to the opposite effect. The less favored one feels rejected.

c. Discriminatory favoritism—giving rewards and resources to a favored one over others. It leads to frustration in the unfavored one, rupturing relationships.

d. Prejudicial favoritism—the unjust expression of compliments, pride, or attention given to extensively someone.

4. There are some slight forms of favoritism in every organization. When favoritism is accentuated, real goals of a group are delayed or defeated.

5. Children are not able select their birth order, gender, appearance or personalities. They have little control over who is selected as the favorite. Intentional favoritism is against God's law of love. 1 Timothy 5:21.

Discussion Questions

1. How do you feel about how favoritism developed in your family?

   In your workplace?

   In your church?

2. Name two of the types of intentional favoritism?

3. Have you experienced intentional favoritism in your life?

Which type was it?

If it was more than one type, what types were they?

What did you do about it (them)?

4. What does God say about favoritism?

Do you agree?

Did the favoritism you experienced draw you away from God?

Chapter 3
The Favored One: The Advantages & Disadvantages

The favored one is selected by a parent or parents even at birth to receive undue attention, praise, rewards and privileges over another child. The child didn't ask for it but just received it because of the factors mentioned in chapters one and two. Dysfunctional favoritism arises when the parent(s) feels so attracted to that child that they invest most of their time, energy and resources into making that child a success. They feel that the child's success is an extension of themselves or their legacy. As a result, they manipulate the child to achieve their goals, which are not necessarily what the child wants or even needs as shown in my story:

When I was born my father, a graduate engineer from MIT, decided he wanted me to follow in his footsteps and become an engineer. When I turned two, he had me wearing a shirt with MIT on it. Later, I received the magazine, *Scientific American,* as a birthday gift and was encouraged to read it and discuss the articles with him. The only problem was that the articles didn't interest me at all. In fact, as I found out later, my mind just doesn't process or remember science. Undeterred, my father persisted by giving me a chemistry set for a birthday saying "You'll really like it." I did actually try some experiments, but not for long.

He constantly urged me toward engineering and attending MIT, where he had graduated with a chemical engineering degree. My love, however, was history, which I just absorbed and even read on my own free time. My mind seemed geared for that, but my father would say, "How can you support yourself on a history teacher's salary?" Believing what my father said, I applied to MIT, but was not immediately accepted. In the meantime, I received a Naval ROTC Scholarship Miami University, which I elected to take. My father allowed me to go there, but insisted that I take a pre-engineering major with the intent of later transferring to an engineering school. The science courses were so demanding, that by my sophomore year, I was on academic probation.

My parents joined me for a fateful meeting at the school to decide what to do. My father continued, "You just need a little tutoring and everything will work out." I didn't believe that at all and made the crucial decision to change my major to economics. To my joy, I excelled getting mostly A's and graduating from Miami. My self-confidence soared, but I felt my father's disdain for my action.

The manipulation by my father created a breach in our relationship that lasted for many years. I felt he really wanted his own agenda and did not have my real interests when he advised me. In fact, he shifted his attention to my sister. Today, I am so relieved that I found my true identity in God, achieved success in the banking world, and in my ministry at Syracuse Teen Challenge. At the end of his life, my father finally recognized my achievements.

This story exemplifies the extent that parents go to achieve their dreams. The failure to consult with the child and learn their abilities and interests can lead to eventual pain for everyone. It points out the need for every child to find their gifting and follow it.

I have already stated that many of us have received preferential treatment at some time in our lives either in our family, church, or workplace. Such reward has some advantages and disadvantages. When dysfunctional favoritism is exercised by the parent or leader, they magnify the advantages and particularly the serious disadvantages of favoritism.

The disadvantages of being the favorite are:

A sense of entitlement. Since the favorite achieves most of his goals, he develops the attitude that he deserves to get most of his desires satisfied by everyone. Others view this as selfishness, which they dislike or resent. Because favorites have not had to live with boundaries in their lives, they mistakenly think they are immune from any discipline or limits. As a result, they often make major mistakes or break the law, which can destroy their achievements and even their lives.

Distant from God. Because favoritism is a sin, favorites can easily become distant from God and his principles. They learn to depend so much on their own abilities that they have little room, or need for God or Jesus in their lives. Paul's approach to such favoritism comes from Roman's 8:5-7: *"Those who live according to the sinful nature have their minds set on what that nature desires; but those who live in accordance with the Spirit have their minds set on what the Spirit desires. The mind of sinful man is death, but the mind controlled by the Spirit is life and peace; the sinful min is hostile to God. It does not submit to God's law, nor can it do so."*

They use worldly wisdom to make their decisions and don't seek God's counsel. Consequently, without boundaries, their morals are often distorted so they do whatever brings success, or pleasure in their eyes.

Manipulate others immorally. Favorites have learned from parents and adults to become very skilled in the art of manipulating others to gain their objectives. As accomplished communicators, they learn how to persuade superiors to give them what they want. In politics, we see them as capable persuaders of large groups of voters. They study and learn different effective techniques of persuasion and use them to get ahead. Outsiders see the phoniness of such tactics and try to stop them, usually with little success. Fame, power, and success are their goals without concern of how one gets there.

Lack of concern for the truth. There is often a bending or distortion of the truth used to reach the goals of the favorite. They have little compunction about lying in order to achieve their desired goals. This lack of concern for what is really true can cause them to even believe their own lies. With such beliefs, serious mistakes are often made that can defeat the favorite in their quest for success.

Others eventually realize the lies and turn against the favorite and his ideas. Soon they don't trust anything the favorite says or does. Proverbs 12:19 speaks of the importance of truth: *"Truthful lips endure forever, but a lying tongue lasts only a moment."* Lying destroys any trust others may have in what the favorite says or does.

Lack of Accountability. Favorites learn quickly that they are not held accountable for their mistakes, or for pushing limits. They feel that they are above any restriction. This occurs because the parent or leader purposely doesn't want to restrict them, and instead excuses their actions. Thus, generally no discipline is given for breaking boundaries. Without feeling godly sorrow for what they have done, favorites will plunge ahead and are certain to commit even greater transgressions. Outsiders see these transgressions and wonder why the parent or leader fails to administer restraint.

Confused identity. Because they have live in sort of a fantasy world created by someone else, their real talents and character have been hidden from them. Who are they really? They have learned to talk and act to be successful by the world's standards. Thus, they have an inflated view of themselves as fostered by the favoring parent or leader. Are they just an actor in the play of life? It's as if their true identity has been taken from them as they struggle to know who they really are. Upon such a realization, they often become depressed with their lives, which can lead to drug addiction or even thoughts of suicide.

Struggles with intimacy. Favorites find no other one can love them as much as the favoring parent loved them as a child. They are so accustomed to their wants being met; they struggle in personal relationships where mutual sharing is so important. They struggle to communicate on a mutual basis. Their main focus is on themselves and their goals, as magnified by dysfunctional favoritism. Consequently, it is very difficult to carry on a mutually sharing personal relationship.

The anguish of loneliness is often the net result of intentional favoritism. Since positive personal relationships are often the greatest joy in most lives, favorites miss out on these meaningful opportunities. Others see this development in the favorite's lives and often feel that this is the payback for all the pain they have suffered from them.

Some of the advantages of being favored are:

Very confident in whatever they seek to accomplish. They come to believe that with very hard work they can overcome almost any challenge. Their brimming self-confidence enables them to take on challenges that others would withdraw from. Failure usually doesn't stop them as they believe so deeply in their abilities.

If they "buy into" the goals of the parent, the parent will try their best to help the favored one achieve those goals. This strong self-confidence helps them become successful when they leave home to face other challenges. However with continued success, they often become conceited, which is contrary to biblical principles. Paul in Philippians 2:3 states: "*Do nothing out of selfish ambition or vain conceit, but in humility consider others better than yourselves.*"

Overachievers. They often gain and expect significant worldly success. Through their laser-like focus and strong determination, they usually achieve their desired goals. With such success, their confidence continues to grow and soon they become leaders in their work, and/or church. Many of our leaders in politics, church, and work are products of such intentional family favoritism.

Skilled charmers. They are socially skilled particularly with those in authority positions. As Ellen Webber Libby states in her book, *The Favorite Child:* ". . . favorite children . . . . can be experts in knowing how to charm people. Charm, an important skill in the art of manipulating people, can emanate from empathy, the ability to identify with someone else's emotional state." She goes on to explain how favorites use these skills to connect with authority figures in a powerful way. Thus, when an authority is seeking those for promotion, advanced learning, or even raises, they will usually choose the favorite one.

Given special privileges. These may include going to bed later as a child, being a class leader in school, or given special training as a member. Many times they are excused from chores at home, or dirty projects. They are given special freedoms usually given to older, or more experienced children, employees, or members. These perks continue to be given to the favorite, who soon learns to expect them on a regular basis. When they don't come continuously, he/she gets depressed, feels slighted, and will often complain to the authority.

Given greater and more rewards than others. These rewards include: a larger allowance, higher salaries, and greater recognition. The authority person often will affirm the child, member or employee with public recognition of their efforts even if others are more deserving. Thus, the favored one looks forward to receiving constant praise.

Optimistic about their future and especially their position in the group. They seek to attain the higher positions no matter what group they are in. Such an optimistic spirit is often contagious with others helping them to become natural leaders. Only in personal relationships do they discover doubt in their abilities as they struggle to share their inner thoughts and feelings.

The advantages of being a favorite are so significant that it is easy to see why children seek to become one. Becoming a favorite in childhood prepares the child for being one in later life and achieving worldly goals and rewards. This success, however, carries a price of emotional problems that can lead to later problems and even great failure. It seems as if being the favorite carries a fatal flaw that has the potential to destroy the accomplishments that the favorite has achieved.

Looking at both the advantages and disadvantages, we get the impression that the favorite gains many short-term advantages, but pays a long-term price. In the end, the degree of dysfunctional favoritism given to a child will often determine their final results. Some favoritism may actually help children gain confidence to face the challenges of the home and world. The story below helps explain this point:

Pam was the first child in her family and became the favorite of her mother from an early age. She liked this position and the continual affirmation from her parents. When her younger sister came along three years later, Pam maintained her favored status. Her mother would tell her "I love you so much. You're so adoring." All these words of love and extra privileges Pam received gave her a strong self-confidence in her abilities.

She loved her younger sister, Emma, so much that she would help her with her challenges. She would try to protect her from punishment from her parents by speaking up in Emma's behalf. If Emma had to stay home as a punishment, Pam would try to do something wrong to get punished and be at home to support her. Pam felt guilty for her favored position, while Emma felt so angry at her mother for her unfavored status.

Pam's self-confidence enabled her to be successful in the business world allowing her to travel around the world. She was away for so long from her mother that her mother started calling her to reconnect. Meantime, Emma, who lived in the same town as their mother, stayed away from her mother out of her pain of being unfavored. Later, Pam's hubris caused her to try drugs, which led to her getting fired, which caused her even greater pain.

Summary:

1. The disadvantages of the favorite are:

a. A sense of entitlement. They deserve to get their desires satisfied. Others see this as selfishness. Favorites think they are immune from discipline. They make major mistakes, which can destroy their achievements and lives.

b. Distant from God. Favoritism is a sin; favorites are distant from God and his principles. They look to their own abilities not to God. Roman's 8:5-7. They depend on worldly wisdom versus godly wisdom.

c. Manipulate others immorally. Favorites are skilled manipulators of others. They learn to persuade superiors to give them what they want. Outsiders see their phoniness. Fame, power and success are their goals without concern of how they get there.

d. Lack of concern for the truth. They distort the truth or lie when seeking their goals. They start to believe their own lies resulting in them making serious mistakes. Others don't trust the favorite and turn against him/her. Proverbs 12:19.

e. Lack of Accountability. Favorites are not held accountable for pushing limits. They feel no godly sorrow for what they have done, so they commit greater transgressions.

f. Confused identity. Their identity is set by their parents without regard for the favorite's abilities. They struggle to find their true identity. Upon realization, they become depressed, which can lead to addiction or suicide.

g. Struggles with intimacy. Favorites find others don't love them as much as their favoring parent. They struggle in personal relationships where mutual sharing is critical. Loneliness is the net result.

2. Advantages of the favorite are:

a. Very confident. Believe that with hard work they can overcome challenges. Their parents help them achieve the parent's goals. They become very successful in the world.

b. Overachievers. They have a laser-like focus to achieve their goals. With success, they become leaders in their church, workplace or politics. Philippians 2:3.

c. Skilled charmers. They are socially skilled with authorities. The authority usually chooses the favorite one for promotion, advanced learning, or raises.

d. Given special privileges. They get special freedoms given older children. The favorite expects them so if they don't come they get depressed, slighted, and complain.

e. Given greater and more rewards. Rewards include: a larger allowance, higher salaries, and greater recognition. The authority person affirms the favorite in public. Favorites expect constant praise.

f. Optimistic. They seek higher positions in every group. Their optimistic spirit is contagious helping them to become leaders.

Discussion Questions

1. Were you favored as a child?

   How did that affect your life for the better?

   How did it affect you for the worse?

2. Whether you were favored or not do you agree with the disadvantages listed?

   Which ones were the most important?

3. Which ones were the biggest advantages?

4. Did you have dysfunctional favoritism in your life?

   How did you deal with it when you became an adult?

Chapter 4

The Unfavored One & The Overlooked One: The Advantages & Disadvantages

You may be unfavored or sometimes what is called least favored status (LFS) receiving the criticism and put downs from parents and later leaders. For some reason whether it be birth order, looks, gender, intelligence, or personality, your parent(s) reject you. Not understanding the reason why, you still strive to find ways to please your parent and gain their approval. Despite your efforts, you still get rejected causing you to feel anger, frustration, and/or depression. You lose confidence in yourself and your abilities. You need to strike out from your parent's control to find God's plan for yourself and your abilities. If not, you could face the real chance of being caught in the prison of resentment for many years or even the rest of your life.

The formula for the unfavored one is:

A parent rejects a child → the parent expresses their rejection of the child → the parent excludes them from the gifts and praise given the favorite → The unfavored still tries to please the authority → the authority still rebuffs the unfavored one causing pain and anger → the unfavored one questions their confidence and abilities → unfavored one flounders in bitterness and lack of success for the rest of their lives. Or ↓

The unfavored one breaks away from the authority's control → the unfavored one seeks God and finds his own identity and abilities → learns to relate well with God and others → becomes successful in both his walk with God and the world.

The equation reflects the fact that the unfavored one develops a strong imprint in his psyche to stay on the path as an unfavored one; however, he/she has the option to find freedom by breaking away and find-ing his/her true self. When that occurs, the unfavored one has the op-portunity to find God and their true identity. It takes great strength to make this break. This is why it is important to lean on God and receive His strength and wisdom.

Unfavored ones feel inner pain toward their parents, who should love and support them, but in fact are actually against them. As a re-sult, they suffer with poor self-esteem and lack of confidence. Regret-tably, too many children fail to climb out of this initial setback and become chronically depressed, resentful of the favorite, their other sib-lings and their parents. Often they struggle to keep up in church groups and later in the workplace.

Because of a weak self-worth, they often end up in poor jobs and unsatisfying marriages. Psychologist Victoria Bedford at the University of Indianapolis has studied unfavored children concluded that ". . . . favoritism negatively affects the relationships, self-esteem and social-ization of unfavored children." Consequently, we see a family that has become divided by dysfunctional favoritism.

"I was not favored and felt alone most of my life" proclaimed Henry, a Teen Challenge student. He went on to reveal how he had been so shunned and rejected by his parents that his anguish continued for most of his life. Even his relatives seemed bent against him. He tried with all of his might to gain their ap-proval, but without success. "I struggled to find what I could do as I tried to please everyone." He never was able to deter-mine what exactly what made him so unappealing.

The torment of his situation caused Henry to join a gang and use drugs for relief. Later he realized he needed Teen Challenge and came to Syracuse Teen Challenge. There he reached out to Christ and found help and solace. "The Lord has no favorites as we are His children and He loves us all" exclaimed Henry after this special revelation of God's love. He went on to tell how the Lord had taken him on a joyous journey of healing by breaking the curse of favoritism and drug addition in his life. Henry had finally received God's comfort of acceptance and peace. Now he knows that his love and direction comes from God and the curse of favoritism has been broken. Today, despite the scars from favoritism his life, he is successful in his life.

We see from this story that if we seek God we can find true healing. The disadvantages of being unfavored occur early in life. These are acerbated if the unfavored one doesn't break away from the negative imprint placed in them from the parents. These are:

Depression. They struggle to find acceptance and love from rejecting parent(s). Why are they being excluded from the love and privileges given to the favored child? They begin to think that something is wrong with them, but they don't know what. The truth is they don't appeal to their parent(s) because they lack certain characteristics of the favorite. They search unsuccessfully to find some way to gain favor with the favoring parent or leader. These fruitless actions lead to emotional stress and eventual depression. This fact was verified by the study, *Mothers' Differentiation and Depressive Symptoms among Adult Children,* published in the April 2010 *Journal of Marriage and Family* confirming that adults unfavored as children frequently experienced depression.

Lower self-confidence. Their skills and abilities are put down on a regular basis by the parent(s) leaving them with a weak self-confidence. They become vulnerable to feeling defeated by the challenges that life brings. It seems as if every day is a struggle to function in their world. As they fail in various challenges, they develop the mind-set that they will never overcome and be successful. Failure upon failure, particularly in the eyes of the parent(s) or leader, leads them into feeling defeated. Even if they do succeed, the authority will often purposely avoid recognizing or encouraging them. They feel caught in a trap of failure.

Struggles with relationships. Often because they have been verbally abused and disregarded by their parents, they are not skilled at communicating their desires and needs. They tend to be shy in interrelationships, which cause them struggles as they try to date and relate with the opposite sex. Socialization becomes a struggle with each relationship. As a result, they may seek only one or two relationships or become loners. They enter into relationships with a defeatist attitude often resulting in them failing.

Develops bitterness. They are angry with their circumstances, their favored sibling, their parent(s) and their other siblings. Too often this anger festers, leading to resentment, and eventual bitterness towards those closest to them. Such bitterness infects those around them and isolates them from real support. They need Christ's help to break this cycle and show them that their unfavored position in the family was a sin.

God cares for each person as Jesus said in Matthew 10:29-31: *"'Are not two sparrows sold for a penny? Yet not one of them will fall to the ground apart from the will of your Father. And even the very hairs of your head are numbered. So don't be afraid; you are worth more than many sparrows.'"* God cares deeply for you. He can remove your bitterness and restore peace in your life.

Greater aggressiveness. Because of their frustration at their situation, unfavored ones may become more aggressive in their actions particularly toward their authorities. In his book, *The Sibling Affect,* Jeffrey Kluger affirms this point from a study of 136 sibling pairs performed by Professor Claire Stocker from the University of Denver. She found ". . . . that unfavored children may turn their disappointment, not only outward, in the form of aggression toward the first-tier brother or sister . . . ."

In dysfunctional families, the unfavored one feels angry at the verbal and even physical abuse they had to absorb. As a result, they strike back particularly when they become teenagers. Their hurt causes them to want to hurt back even against others who were not involved in the abuse. In church or their workplace, their aggression is often expressed in a passive-aggressive ways like working slowly on purpose or doing sloppy work.

The advantages of being the unfavored one usually occur later in life and especially after they have broken away from their favoring parent and find Christ in their lives. These are:

True to themselves. They are not burdened by the often unrealistic expectations of the favoring parent(s). Consequently, they have the freedom to be who they really are without pretending. When they find their own identity and talents they will be able to excel. They are not beholding to the favoring parent, or later their boss. If they don't break away, they very well may never find their true identity.

Drawn closer to Christ. Because they have suffered so much, they are open to turn to Christ for support and direction. Christ understands their suffering and is able to minister to them in the most effective way. They feel His healing touch in their lives and are often drawn to Him becoming dedicated Christians. Thus, they seek a relationship with Christ as their dear friend and companion. Paul in Romans 8:17 shows how suffering brings us closer to Christ: *"Now if we are children, then we are heirs—heirs of God and co-heirs with Christ. If indeed we share in his sufferings in order that we may also share in his glory."*

Have deeper personal relationships. Their suffering helps them to become sensitive to others suffering, which is critical to building deep relationships. The man in the story above married an unfavored one reflecting his compassion and had a positive relationship. They tend to have a greater desire for better personal relationships over worldly success. These meaningful connections with others give them a feeling of personal accomplishment.

May achieve greater success. Favorites are so often controlled by the parent's desire to achieve their goals, which may be completely different from the favorite's identity or ability. Unfavored ones are not fettered with such expectations, so they can seek their own goals once they free themselves from believing parental criticism. Ellen Webber Libby affirms this in her book, *The Favorite Child,* "*Not* being the favorite may be painful to the child but may assure health and success in adulthood by insulating the person against tragedy." By overcoming the lies of parental criticism, they find the truth about their abilities. Then, they can move on to achieve their own goals and find positive personal satisfaction and approval.

In summary, the unfavored one, particularly from a dysfunctional family, faces a difficult life unless they can break away from their parent(s). This position is affirmed by Jeffery Kluger in his book, who quoted "Psychologist Victoria Bedford of the University of Indianapolis has studied favoritism extensively: ". . . looking at the impact of what she calls the LFS (least favored status) on children's relationships with other family members, self-esteem maintenance, socialization, and later functioning in the world. No matter how she broke down her data, it all told the same thing. 'My conclusion is how horrible favoritism is to siblings,' she says flatly and sibs often agree.'"

THE OVERLOOKED ONE

"My parents never told me that they loved me!" Antonio said sadly. He was a young Mexican-American student at Syracuse Teen Challenge who was a middle child in a family of six children. "Whenever my youngest brother and I did something wrong, he would never get blamed. All the criticism fell on me." The youngest brother was the favorite in the family and seemed to never get corrected.

The unfairness of this situation angered Antonio, who soon sought affirmation outside the family in the Mexican gangs on the west coast. They gave him protection and initial affirmation. Later, he realized all they wanted was his efforts to build power and money for the leaders. By then, Antonio was into drugs which ultimately led him to Syracuse Teen Challenge and eventually a relationship with Christ. Today, he is pressing in to change his life for God and discover what plans God has for him. "I want to be a godly father to my two young boys." However, his wife doesn't trust him because of his past frequent drug use and she doesn't talk to him very much. He is depending on Christ to help him change into a new godly husband and overcome the sting of being an unloved, overlooked child.

The overlooked ones are those children, workers, or members whose parents, bosses or authorities are neither attracted to, nor disliked by them. They seem to be invisible or ignored by the authorities in their lives. Therefore, they can easily develop an abandonment feeling. They are usually the middle children in a family unless they are the gender-preferred child. At work, they are the average employee who doesn't create disturbances and at church, they are the average parishioner who doesn't cause problems. The authorities neither give them praise nor criticism, but usually take them for granted. In dysfunctional families, the overlooked one will often appreciate their unseen position as they avoid the scrutiny of the unfavored one and the intensity of the favored one. Yet deep inside they yearn for some relationship with the parent or authority.

The formula for the overlooked one is:

A parent ignores a child → the parent neither expresses criticism nor praises the child → they are excluded from the gifts, promotions, and

praise given the favorite → The overlooked one tries to please the authority to get some attention → the authority continues to not give them any attention causing greater pain and anger → they try getting negative attention → the overlooked one questions their self-confidence and abilities → (dysfunctional families) the overlooked one may become caught in a prison of bitterness and lack of success for the rest of his life. Or ↓

The overlooked one breaks away from the authority's control → the overlooked one seeks God and finds his own identity and abilities → learns to relate well with God and others → becomes successful in both his walk with God and the world.

In the dysfunctional family, the formula is similar for the unfavored one except that the overlooked one is not as emotionally damaged. Still, breaking away by the overlooked one and seeking God is a crucial step in the healing process. God knows their true identity and guides them in selecting the best choices for their life whether it be marriage and/or job.

The overlooked one senses their ignored position and may strive for attention, even if it is negative. Thus, they may purposely become aggressive by picking fights with a parent as shown in the following story.

April was a middle child with an older sister and two younger brothers. She was three years younger than her sister and five years older than her oldest brother. Her sister was very bright and skilled with her words so that she could often get what she wanted. The mother's favorite was her youngest brother. The unfavored one was her oldest brother who received constant harsh criticism from their father.

Her mother never gave her any attention, but instead focused all her energies on her younger brother. Since everyone else in the family seemed to be getting some form of attention, April felt left out. She refused to be overlooked any longer, so she purposely began to pick fights with her father on a regular basis. It was amazing to see them both go at it. If one said black the other said white and vice versa as they both stubbornly refused to compromise. They seemed to be constantly at polar opposites. April disliked her father because of his harsh treatment towards her, his rigid opinions, and fixed ideas. As April aged; it became obvious to her that they could find little in agreement. Later in life she realized, "I acted this way with my father just to get at least some attention, even if it was negative."

We see the above true story that the craving of the overlooked child for attention from the parents is taken to great lengths. In later life, April gave up trying to get attention from her father and sought it from other more reliable sources like God, her husband, and dear friends.

The disadvantages of the overlooked one are increased if the overlooked child does not break away from the family. These are:

Weak self-esteem. They usually lack the affirmation and the encouragement from their parents as a child so they are uncertain and tentative about their abilities and skills. This weak self-esteem can hurt their ability to succeed in church and in the workplace. They will hold back on proposing their ideas and opinions. Depending upon their personalities, they will usually start to break out in their teenage years and seek their own path and take on more risk. There, with God's help, they will find their true abilities, achieve success, and greater self-esteem.

Stay in destructive relationships. Because of their intense loyalty they will continue to stay in abusive and hurtful relationships. They want the relationship to succeed so much that they overlook the pain they are receiving. As a result, they feel that they can make the relationship work if they only tried harder. Without their spouse also wanting the same goal, such efforts will prove to be futile.

Overly influenced by their friends. Their parents were usually emotionally distant from them so they turn to their friends for advice. This advice is often ineffective or even destructive as they lack the wisdom of adult experience. They will tend to want to be with their friends more than their family. If their friends are evil, their sin can affect the overlooked one significantly in a destructive way. They feel emotionally distant from their parents and siblings causing them to often stay away from them for long periods or even their whole lives.

The advantages of being an overlooked one come later in life and are:

Freedom to find themselves. Being overlooked can give a child a greater sense of freedom to pursue other more gratifying sources of affirmation outside the family. They find these sources in good Christian friends and wise adults who can lead them to find God and truth in their lives. They don't have the burdens of being favored or unfavored with their heavy downsides.

The key for their success is not to become stuck in the resentment for being overlooked. They need to discover that they are a child of God who has a plan for them. As Jeremiah 29:11 states: "'*I know the plans I have for you, plans to prosper you and not to harm you,' declares the Lord 'plans to give you hope and a future.'*"

Loyalty in their relationships. They demonstrate great loyalty to: their friends, spouses, and organizations that they belong to. Catherine Salmon, associate professor at the University of Redlands in California confirms this in her book, *The Secret Power of Middle Children: How Middleborns Can Harness Their Unexpected and Remarkable Abilities,* "If you are the one who is often overlooked, you get used to really working at building and sacrificing to make a relationship work." As a result, they usually have less divorce and infidelity in their marriages. Also, their marriages enjoy greater satisfaction.

Good negotiators. They seem to have a skill at negotiating difficult challenges. As overlooked children, they experience the disruption caused by the oldest one and the cries for attention from the youngest one. They seek harmony in their relationships and strive to work out difficulties in relationships.

Tend to be creative. They develop unique thinking and creative abilities that they can use to become successful in their lives. Catherine Salmon in her book affirms this: "They're more willing to take that leap of faith and believe in things that are somewhat unproven. A different way of thinking and a willingness to entertain crazy ideas often leads to innovation." Steve Jobs, the major founder and former CEO of Apple, was such an example of a middle child with an amazing creativity that led to great innovation in cell phones and computers.

Are usually patient. As children, they learn to wait for their turn after the firstborn gets his privileges and the last-born gets his attention. They learn the skill of delayed gratification, which can serve them well later in life when patience is important. This skill is also very helpful in building close interpersonal relationships where patient listening creates close connections.

The overlooked ones often end up becoming the most successful of the three types particularly in personal relationships. They have an opportunity to succeed in the world if they break away from their initial abandonment by their parents. With God directing them, they have the opportunity to succeed.

In summarizing the three types, the favorite will often find initial success in the family, church and work. However, being the favorite often has dangerous defects that have the potential to harm them and/or their accomplishments. The unfavored carries a heavy burden of emotional pain of rejection from their parents. This debilitating yoke can easily be carried into adulthood and can become an incapacitating bitterness, unless they break free and find God's plan for their lives.

The overlooked one struggles to find attention from the positive sources that can affirm him/her. Once they break from the disregard of their parents they have the opportunity for a successful life. What is critical is for each type to discover a belief in Christ for their lives. He will help them find their true identity and His plans will bless their lives regardless of their parent's expectations for them. Then each type will find true contentment.

Summary:

1. The unfavored one receives the rejection from their parents for characteristics they can't change. They strive to please their parents, but get rejected and feel anger, frustration, and/or depression.

2. They lose confidence in themselves. Once they leave their parent's control and find God's plan, they find success. Otherwise, they get caught in the prison of resentment. The formula for the unfavored one is: **A parent rejects a child → the parent expresses their criticism of the child → they exclude them from the gifts, promotions, and praise given the favorite → The unfavored one still tries to please the authority → the authority still rejects the unfavored causing greater pain and anger → the unfavored one questions their self-confidence and abilities → unfavored one flounders in bitterness and lack of success for the rest of their lives. Or ↓**

The unfavored one breaks away from the authority's control → the unfavored one seeks God and finds his own identity and abilities → learns to relate well with God and others → becomes successful in both his walk with God and the world.

3. The disadvantages of being unfavored usually occur early in life are:

a. Depression. They don't understand why they are excluded from parental love. The reason is they don't have the favorite's characteristics. They search unsuccessfully gain favor with the parent, which leads often to depression.

b. Lower self-confidence. Their abilities are regularly put down by the parent(s) creating questions in them about their abilities and a weak self-confidence. They are vulnerable to feeling defeated by the challenges. If they succeed, the authority doesn't recognize them.

c. Struggles with relationships. They are not skilled communicators and are shy in relationships. So they seek one or two relationships, or become loners. They enter into relationships with a defeatist attitude resulting in failure.

d. Develop bitterness. They are angry with, the favored sibling, their parent(s) and other siblings. This anger festers, leading to bitterness towards their family, infects those around them, and isolates them from support. They need Christ to break this cycle and show them that favoritism is a sin. Matthew 10: 29-31.

e. Greater aggressiveness. Because of their frustration, unfavored ones may become more aggressive toward their authorities. In dysfunctional families, the unfavored one feels angry at their abuse. As teenagers, they strike back.

4. The advantages of the unfavored come about later in their lives are:

a. True to themselves. Not burdened by their parent's expectations they have freedom to find their true identity. They are not beholding to parents, but God. If they fail to break away, they may never find their identity. They achieve little workplace success.

b. Drawn closer to Christ. Because of suffering, they turn to Christ who ministers to them. They feel His healing touch and become dedicated Christians. Romans 8:17.

c. Have deeper personal relationships. Their suffering helps them become sensitive to others that are hurting. They have better personal relationships than worldly success.

d. May achieve greater success. Unfavored ones are not fettered with high expectations and seek their own goals. Once they stop believing the parent's criticism, they find the truth about their abilities. Then they achieve satisfaction and approval.

The Overlooked One

1. The overlooked ones are neither attracted to nor disliked by their parents. They are ignored by the authorities and feel abandoned. They are usually middle children. In dysfunctional families, they avoid the scrutiny of the unfavored one and the intensity of the favored one.

2. The formula for the overlooked one is: **An parent ignores a child → the parent neither expresses criticism nor praises the child → they are excluded from the gifts and praise given the favorite → The overlooked one tries to please the authority to get some attention → the authority continues to not pay attention causing greater pain and anger → they try getting negative attention → the overlooked one questions their self-confidence and abilities → (dysfunctional families) the overlooked one may become caught in a prison of bitterness and lack of success for the rest of his life. Or ↓**
The overlooked one breaks away from the authority's control → the overlooked one seeks God and finds his own identity → learns to relate well with God and others → becomes successful in both his walk with God and the world.

3. The overlooked one senses they are ignored and strive for attention even if negative. They may purposely pick fights with their parent(s). The disadvantages of the overlooked one are:

a. Weak self-esteem. They are not affirmed by their parents and become uncertain. This weak self-esteem hurts their ability to succeed. As a teenager, they seek their own path and search for God's help.

b. Stay in destructive relationships. Because of their loyalty, they will stay in hurtful relationships. They want the relationship to succeed so they overlook their pain and try to make it work. Without their spouse's similar desire, such efforts are futile.

c. Overly influenced by their friends. Their parents are distant so they turn to friends for advice. Their advice is ineffective as they lack life experience. Overlooked ones tend to stay with friends over their family. Their evil friends can cause them to sin.

4. The advantages of an overlooked one are:

a. Freedom to find themselves. They pursue other sources of affirmation outside the family. They find these in good Christian friends who lead them to God. The key is to not become stuck in resentment for being overlooked. They find that they are a child of God.

b. Loyalty in relationships. They demonstrate great loyalty to: their friends, spouses, and organizations. They have less divorce and infidelity in their marriages.

c. Good negotiators. They are skilled negotiators of difficult challenges. They seek harmony in their relationships and workout difficulties. They often develop unique creative abilities that become successful. Steve Jobs.

d. Are usually patient. As children, they learn to wait their turn after the other children. The skill of delayed gratification helps them in later life with relationships.

5. Overlooked ones can become the most successful of the three types particularly in personal relationships. They need to find God and have Him direct them.

Discussion Questions

1. Were or are you now the unfavored one in your family?

   Did or does that make you angry at your parent(s)?

2. Have you broken away from your parent's control?

   Have you found Christ in your life?

3. Which advantages and disadvantages do you find in your life?

4. Were you the overlooked one in your family?

   Were you angry with that position?

   What have you done about it?

Chapter 5

Destructive Pride:
A Major Element of the Favorite

"God opposes the proud but gives grace to the humble." (James 4:6)

Pride is defined by Webster's New International Dictionary as "inordinate self-esteem: an unreasonable conceit of superiority (as in talents, beauty, wealth, rank)." Pride is one of the main characteristics of the favored child since he/she received most everything they desired. As a baby, they got what they wanted the most, the full attention and love of their parent(s). In turn, the parents too often use their influence to control the child's direction in a way that enhances the parent's reputation called intentional favoritism. Also, the child is given most every physical possession that they want plus the constant affirmation from their parents for their activities. All this adulation breeds a self-confident attitude in the child, but also has a dark side of intense pride in themselves or an attitude of conceit.

This voracious pride creates the expectations in us that we deserve to get all we can without limitation. We become very concerned with our desire to have a dominant status in our families, church, and workplace. This self-centered aspiration to be in charge of our lives is similar to the same sin that Satan committed when he wanted to be equal with God. Dr. Les Carter and Dr. Frank Minirth in their, *Anger Workbook,* expand on this point: ". . . God had given Adam (who represents each of us) the instruction to be free while refraining from the temptation to be God-like in applying knowledge. But in choosing to defy God's command, Adam took control of his own life. The inner push that prompted him to do this was his pride." Drs. Carter and Minirth go on to talk about "being in Adam" as our original sin. C.J. Mahaney and Joshua Harris in their book, *Humility: True Greatness,* expand on this: "Why does God hate pride so passionately? Here's why: Pride is when sinful human beings aspire to the status and position of God and refuse to acknowledge their dependence on Him." We all carry some pride in our lives so it is our responsibility to overcome it on a daily basis. As a result of such hubris, we feel that we have the right to break the boundaries established by the family and society for our protection.

Those of us caught in egotistic pride have a noticeable lack of concern for others and their needs so that we lack empathy and compassion. Such a narcissistic attitude makes it difficult for us to connect with our siblings and potential friends. Dr. Les Carter highlights this point in his book, *The Anger Trap:* "This egotistic pride can be defined as the preoccupation with self. It is pushed along by the urge to satisfy personal cravings, preferences, or desires. It provokes the individual to become so inwardly focused that the ability to tend to the feelings and needs of others is lost."

Emily grew up in a family of three other siblings. As the first child she was indulged by her parents with love and attention, which she relished. Her mother would say," Emily is so smart and quick to understand everything I tell her." Thus, Emily became the favorite in the family. She maintained that position despite having two younger siblings due to her strong personality and verbal skills. She would dominate her siblings so that her needs always had priority. Conceit crept into her attitude as she expected special treatment from her parents. They would give in to her demands, which only fed her appetite for more things and privileges. Sadly, Emily's pride was getting out of control and becoming conceit.

One day at school, one of her fourth grade classmates had a new cell phone, which she coveted. Instead of asking her parents for one, on an impulse she stole it. A teacher caught her and reported her crime to the principal and then to her parents. Emily felt no remorse for what she had done, but only that she had been caught. Her heart was becoming so hardened by her pride that she could admit no wrong. Her parents only told her not to do it again. As she got older she decided to experiment with drugs and became addicted to heroin. This strong drug caused her to steal to get money for it. Emily's life spiraled downward until she was arrested. It was then that her parents realized she had gone too far. They put her into a women's Teen Challenge. There she was deeply humbled and finally relinquished her old self over to God and her self-centeredness left her.

We see in the story how destructive pride can literally destroy a young life. This pride is present in all of us and can develop into dangerous conceit, which can control us. Thus, we have a spiritual disease that can only be healed by seeking God's help.

Christ is very aware of how conceit can destroy our lives. He knows that the end result of selfishness is great pain and danger. To prevent this event, He wants us to shift our focus off of ourselves onto others. The apostle Paul in Philippians 2:3-4 admonishes us to: *"Do nothing out of selfish ambition or vain conceit, but in humility value others above yourselves. Each of you should look not only to your own interests, but also to the interests of others."* By becoming other-focused, we learn to care for others' needs more than our own. Thereby, we diminish our inherent self-seeking attitudes by giving of ourselves to those in need. As we start to care for others, we develop a greater sense of compassion for them and their concerns. The by-product of this action is the blessing that we are better able to connect with other people at a personal level that builds close relationships.

Another outgrowth of pride is a narcissism resulting in greater destructive anger in our lives. Drs. Carter and Minirth address pride in their workbook: "This inborn sinful nature accompanies all inappropriate forms of anger. Whether we shout or ridicule or criticize or withdraw in abusive silence we nurse the thought, *'Why can't people be what I say they should be?'"* The aggressive angry person reflects pride in his/her forceful intent to impose their feelings on someone without respectful interaction. Likewise, the passive-aggressive angry person subtly tries to impose indirectly their anger on someone by being purposely late or slow in doing a job. Prideful anger is revealed in Christian circles using what I call, "hostile silence" (also called the silent treatment). This form of anger occurs when someone is angry with someone so they stop talking or relating with that person. The initiator mistakenly believes that they are really hurting the other person by not relating, while in reality that person just goes on with their life. Such actions may go on for years.

Pride is especially demonstrated in conflict when one party confronts another with something hurtful that they did, but the second party immediately reverses the conversation to something that the first party did to them. This reversal process reflects the prideful attitude of the second party who refuses to accept correction. Some people use reversal as a defense mechanism every time someone tries to correct them. In fact, we had a student at Syracuse Teen Challenge who so constantly used reversal that we called him "Mr. Reversal." Unfortunately, he left the program early and I don't know if he ever got the help he sought. Without accepting correction, a person will never be able to truly change and get better.

HUMILITY—A SOURCE OF TRUE CHANGE

"... declares the Lord, This is the one I esteem: he who is humble and contrite in spirit..." Isaiah 66:2

Humbleness is defined by Webster's as, "Having a low opinion of one's own importance or merits." It is the opposite of pride in that the person does not take credit for his abilities or achievements, but instead gives God the credit. Drs. Carter and Minirth in their workbook speak to this: "The trait that keeps us in submission to God is humility. The opposite of pride, it is a lack of self-preoccupation and a willingness to acknowledge personal limits." Because of our inherent prideful nature, we must be intentional in our desire to develop a humble attitude in our hearts. I have found that, when I am blessed by success, I need to give God the glory for it. As Deuteronomy 8:18 says: *"But remember the Lord your God, for it is he who gives you the ability to produce wealth, and so confirms his covenant, which he swore to your forefathers, as it is today."* Then He drains the conceit from our hearts and we fully recognize that we can do nothing without God's help and direction. Humbleness also frees us from the trap of thinking we are alone and must overcome every challenge through our own ability. This act of submission gives us new confidence and freedom from the stress of depending upon our own performance. Humbleness is reflected in a person's actions such as:

Serving others first. Our thoughts and actions are focused on others needs more than our own. We think of ourselves as part of a community and compelled to help others with whom we are connected. This other-preoccupation helps us to not only avoid greed and selfishness, but instead blesses us with a feeling of God's joy in our hearts.

Becoming more empathetic. Webster's definition of empathy is: "the capacity for participating in or a vicarious experiencing of another's feelings, violations, or ideas . . ." Empathy is when we have such a deep care for someone else so that we connect with what they say and feel. Empathy enables us to develop closer connections with others resulting in deep relationships with them.

Accepting personal limits. We realize that we are fallible beings with many weaknesses including a penchant for pride. Thus, we look to Jesus for help and are so grateful to Him for showing us how to be humble. We accept that we are a work-in-process seeking to become more like Jesus until we die.

Provides us with strength. Contrary to what society thinks, humbleness is not being a milk toast. Jesus gives us the fortitude to stand up strongly for Him and His principles. This point is echoed by

Dr. Les Carter in his book when he says: "What would you think if I told you that humility represents ultimate strength? Humble people are not marshmallows; they are poised to be highly influential leaders. In fact, humility is the only path to true greatness."

Respectful in his words and actions. Because of our close relationship with Jesus, we want to emulate Him by respecting others. In effect, we are His representatives on earth working for His plan. We do this by being respectful with our own words and actions. Such respect reflects a caring attitude for others, which draws them closer to Jesus.

Patience. We are patient in our interactions with others by listening closely to them and by accepting their foibles. Again we are replicating what Jesus does for us and did in the Bible. Patience is an act of love for the other person.

Able to make real changes in our lives. When we listen to the correction by the Holy Spirit, this conviction compels us to make significant changes in our life. We realize our limitations and humbly seek Christ's direction for our lives.

God gives us His grace. We are blessed by God's favor in all of our endeavors. He gives us access to His power to overcome fear and challenges in our lives. Thus, we are willing and able to embark on new ventures for God. Grace enables us to overcome the fear of possible failure and rejection.

C.J Mahaney and Joshua Harris in their book. *Humility: True Greatness*, speak about grace: "God is decisively drawn to humility. The person who is humble is the one who draws God's attention, and in this sense, drawing His attention means also drawing His grace—His unmerited kindness." As we humble ourselves, God's grace will start to flow throughout our lives in all our relationships so that others are positively influenced.

Jesus in Mathew 23:10 tells us: *"'Whoever exalts himself will be humbled, and whoever humbles himself will be exalted.'"* Thus, if we don't humble ourselves, then God has a way of humbling us as prideful people. He will allow our hubris to cause us to stumble and fall over issues in our lives.

Summary:

1. Pride is defined in Webster's as "inordinate self-esteem: an unreasonable conceit of superiority (as in talents, beauty, wealth, rank)." It is a major characteristic of the favored person. Pride starts when a baby gets the full attention and love of their parent(s) over the child's life excluding the other children.

2. Parents use their influence to control the child's thoughts and actions to enhance the parent's reputation intentional favoritism. They give their child everything they want plus their affirmation creating a self-confident, prideful child.

3. Pride creates unlimited expectations. Egotistic pride was Satan's original sin and later in Adam. It is inherent in all of us that we want to be our own gods. We feel we can break parental and society's boundaries.

4. Egotistic pride is lack of concern for others, lack of empathy, which makes it difficult for us to connect with siblings and friends.

5. Conceit can destroy our lives or cause great pain. Christ wants us to shift our focus from ourselves to others. Philippians 2:3-4. We are called to diminish our self-seeking attitudes by giving to the needy and thereby develop compassion.

6. Destructive anger develops from conceit. The aggressive angry person reflects pride when they forcefully impose their feelings on some-

one else. The passive-aggressive angry person subtly tries to impose indirectly their intentions on someone. Hostile silence, a form of pride, occurs when someone stops relating with them. The initiator mistakenly believes that they are hurting the other person, but the other person goes on with their life.

7. Pride is demonstrated in conflict when one party confronts another about something hurtful they did, but the second party immediately reverses the conversation to something that the first party did to them. They don't accept correction and instead use reversal every time.

Humility—A Source of True Change

1. Humbleness is defined as, "Having a low opinion of one's own importance or merits." It is the opposite of pride when the person does not take credit for his achievements.

2. Humbleness is a daily walk to overcome pride in our hearts. We intentionally give God the glory for His helping us to achieve our success. Humbleness frees us from the trap of thinking we are alone. By submitting to God, He gives us new confidence. Humbleness is shown in the following:

a. Serving others first. Focus on others' needs. Other-preoccupation helps us to only avoid selfishness and blesses us with God's joy in our hearts. The definition of empathy is: "the capacity for participating in or a vicarious experiencing of another's feelings, violations, or ideas . . ."

b. Accepting personal limits. We realize that we have many weaknesses including pride. We accept that we are a work-in-process seeking to become more like Jesus.

c. Provides us with strength. Humbleness is not being a milk toast as Jesus gives us fortitude to stand up for Him. It gives us the ability to become influential leaders.

d. Respectful in his words and actions. We want to emulate Jesus by respecting others through our words and actions.

e. Patience. We are patient with others by listening to them and by accepting them. We are replicating what Jesus does for us.

f. Able to make real change in our lives. Listening to correction and convicted to change, we make significant life changes. We realize our limitations and humbly seek Christ's direction for our lives.

g. God gives us His grace. God blesses us with His grace and His favor in our endeavors. He gives us His power to overcome challenges and start new ventures. Grace overcomes our fear of failure and rejection. God's grace flows through our lives and our relationships.

3. **Matthew 23:10.** God will humble us as prideful people. He may allow our hubris to cause us to fall over simple things.

Discussion Questions

1. As a favored child did you find egotistic pride has crept into your life? What are you doing about it?

2. Has narcissism developed in your life? How has it affected your relationships?

3. Read Philippians 2:3-4 and Romans 12:3. How do these verses affect your life?

4. Do you find that you have an anger problem? Could pride be a part of the reason?

5. Have you found humbleness in Christ in your life? What manifestations of God did you discover in your life?

Chapter 6
Favoritism from Childhood to Teenage Years

The story of favoritism starts in the home when the couple gets their first child. The arrival of the new baby brings immediate change into the household life as each partner must focus on the many needs of the new arrival. While usually father and mother each adopt a role in the care of the new child, it is usually the mother that takes on the primary caretaker role. Each parent is fascinated by this new creation and each one gives the new child much of their attention with time, photos, and love, which the child soaks up. As Linda Sonna PhD states in her book, *The Everything Parent's Guide To Raising Siblings,* "They are equally fastidious about every aspect of their firstborn's health and welfare. First-time parents are prone to devour child-rearing articles and compare notes with other parents."

The baby craves all that attention and even more as he/she begins to feel special or favored by their parents. Physical appearance has such a strong influence in determining the favorite. The mother, as the primary caregiver, often takes the lead in selecting the favored one, as my mother did with me when she was strongly attracted to my appearance. The first child has a strong advantage of becoming the favored one since there is no competition. This preference for the firstborn was confirmed by a study conducted by Catherine Conger, Professor of Human Development at the University of California. In the study of 384 sibling pairs, she concluded that 65% of the mothers and 70% of the fathers favored the first child.

While appearance is a strong determinant in selecting the favored one, gender is a close second. Having the same gender as the baby creates strong ties with the same gender parent, because of their mutual interests. Coupled with this is the parent's desire to leave their legacy with a similar gender child. In three children families having different sexes, gender usually becomes the deciding factor on which child is favored. There is, however, a frequent pattern of cross-gendered preferences where the parents value the traits of their opposite-sexed children. This situation is particularly true when that child exhibits the characteristics of that parent. There can be a strong appeal to a father whose daughter is very athletic or an artistic son to a mother.

A child's personality also plays an important role in selecting a favorite. The child with outgoing and verbal abilities often gains the advantage in the favoritism battle. Usually, the first-born develops these skills from interacting with their parents before the second child arrives. However, if the personality of the first child is withdrawn and their verbal skills are slow to develop, a verbal second child particularly a girl, can appeal to the parents and become the favorite. Their social ability draws the parents towards that child.

God wants us to love each of our children as a special blessing from Him as Solomon writes in Psalm 127:3: *"Sons are a heritage from the Lord, children are a reward from him."* Each child has been given their own unique abilities by God, who has a special plan for their future. As Psalm 40:5 confirms: *"But the plans of the Lord stand firm forever, the purposes of his heart through all generations."* Thus, He doesn't see us as a favored one, unfavored one or overlooked one, but as equally favored, but with different god-given abilities. As parents, He wants us to treat our children kindly as His special gifts that are in our care and teaching for a short time. Carol Kuykendall in her book, *Five-Star Families,* elaborates on several of the gifts from God that children give to parents: "We get a second chance to fill in the holes left over from our own childhood. Then a 'gift of wonder' next the 'gift of humility' next the 'gift of childlike faith' and finally the 'gift of growing better.'"

Dan and Alma, married in their mid-twenties, had Kate within their first year. She had a winsome smile that appealed to everyone who interacted with her. Her parents, like most new parents, devoted careful efforts to make sure she was changed, fed, and received plenty of attention. Soon numerous photos of Kate appeared on Facebook as her parents recorded every new development from her first steps to her first words. Alma, drawn by her smile, stated, "Kate's just so cute when she smiles!" She quickly developed an ability to verbally express her desires. Soon she excelled through preschool and into first grade. She felt compelled to do her school work at a high level of achievement. Overall, Kate felt content and secure in her world with her parents favoring her as the first-born.

In this story, we see the characteristics of being a first-born child, which gives them the initial advantage of becoming the favorite:

No competition. Parents have a natural affinity to appreciate their first child. They marvel over this new creation and dote over him/her making sure they are good, responsible parents. Every step of progress is noted and recorded with the child receiving affirmation. If there are twins, the parents try to acknowledge both, but a favorite often emerges.

Perfectionism. This attribute often comes from the parents, who are perfectionist in their approach to caring for the new baby. They want to do everything by the textbook so they are considered fine parents. The child internalizes this approach in their psyche and often become a perfectionist themselves when they reach adulthood.

Strong desires to please their parents. First-born try hard to please their parents and usually get rewarded for doing so. The strongest reward is affirmation and positive attention from the parents, which means much more to the child than candy or goodies.

Increased verbal ability. This skill is the by-product of the parents spending time talking with their first-born more than they do subsequent children. This training time with the child enables them to learn and develop language skills. The parents are intent on helping the child become a success in school and life as a reflection on them. The favoritism shown is natural and should provide the child with some of the advantages of favoritism such as greater focus, determination and confidence to succeed. It is possible that intentional favoritism could arise as with my father's intentions to push me to become an MIT engineer.

Going on with our story.

Then Kate's world was turned upside down with the arrival of her brother, Edwin. He was sickly with physical problems requiring much of her parent's attention. The family's dynamics had changed and Kate quickly recognized it. She now had strong competition for her parent's attention, which the child recognizes as parental love. At first she viewed her brother as a large doll, except he kept moving. Her initial reaction was to regress back to being a baby. Although she had been toilet trained for several years, she began to have "accidents" and even requested a diaper.

As Alma cared for Edwin, Kate watched as her mother would tell her what she was doing. Gradually, Kate was learning how to care for Edwin as she helped alongside her mother. As her mother saw that Kate was becoming responsible in her care of Edwin, she asked her: "Kate, please watch over baby while I do something." Kate felt a surge of importance and a new more important role in the family. Kate initially had feelings of sibling rivalry with Edwin that caused her to commit subtle, but occasional attacks on him. However, as Edwin grew and began to walk and talk, Kate discovered she had a new playmate. Her feelings of sibling rivalry faded and a new sense of sibling bonding occurred. They had fun making up games together as you could see them drawing closer together.

Then Alma began to show increased favoritism towards

Edwin on a daily basis. Kate in an effort to counter balance this painful favoritism, she gravitated to her father for attention. Despite her attempts he stayed aloof. The specter of intentional favoritism had crept into the family and Kate struggled with its effect on her.

We have seen several new aspects that have developed:

Parent's attention shifts to a new child. This change is particularly true when a baby has difficulties of any kind. Because a baby's natural needs demands attention, a baby born with difficulties only increases those demands from the parents. Often the first child doesn't always understand this situation and usually resents the shift of the parent's attention away from her/him.

The first child's regression. This action is a cry for attention from a young child who doesn't fully grasp the greater needs required by this new addition. They miss all the attention that they formerly received. Linda Sonna PhD in her book describes this phase: "This is a common reaction to having to cope with so many changes when a new sibling arrives. Potty-trained children may start having accidents." She goes on to recommend that the parents have the older child help feed the baby its bottle.

Ask the first-born to take on responsibilities with the new child. Parents frequently ask the first child to do this as a means of helping them. They are, however, building a sense of responsibility into the child, which helps them be responsible as they move into other settings. Giving the older child increasing responsibilities keeps them engaged and gives them a certain status. I remember being asked several times to do this with my sister which caused me to feel more mature. Later as the child becomes a teenager, they tend to resent these requests as they strongly prefer to be with their friends.

In this part of the story, we see the following elements related to favoritism occurring:

Fluid favoritism. A concept developed by Dr. Kent Ravenscroft, a child psychiatrist and professor at Georgetown University, that every child should have the opportunity to become the favorite. Often this occurs with the child in the baby to toddler stages, but may occur later depending upon the parent's preferred developmental stage for the child. Such an approach gives each child an opportunity at being in the spotlight and gaining some of the advantages of being a favorite for a while.

Sibling rivalry. The children fight with each other for their parent's attention, toys, food, and who gets something first. Though sibling rivalry is thought to be innate in children, studies show that it develops to a greater degree in chaotic homes or where competition is fostered by the parent(s). Favoritism for one child by a parent enhances sibling rivalry. When sibling rivalry is rampant, undermining each other becomes a goal.

Bonding. This action between children is a natural and desired step to reducing the effects of partiality. Bonding develops when children feel a personal closeness with each other from them overcoming mutual challenges or through shared experiences. Depending upon the parents, bonding can be enhanced as the children watch their parents interact with each other. Strong bonding between the children can defeat attempts by a parent to favor one child. In fact, the favored child will often reject such an attempt and even feel guilty about it.

Intentional favoritism or dysfunctional favoritism. When a parent's attention is devoted to one child and controls that child's performance to achieve the parent's personal goals. As a part of this process, a special bond develops between the parent and the favored one who receives constant benefits (preferential favoritism) for submitting to the actions of the parent. Another element is comparative favoritism whereby the parent publicly uplifts the abilities of the favorite over those of their other children.

God is against favoritism particularly intentional favoritism as in Acts 10:34: "*Then Peter began to speak: 'I now realize how true it is that God does not show favoritism . . .'*" He calls us to love and treat each child with respect. The apostle John in 1 John 4:7 highlights this point: "*Dear friends, let us love one another for love comes from God. Everyone who loves has been born of God and knows God. Whoever does not love does not know God, because God is love.*" Also respect found in 1 Peter 2:17: "*Show proper respect to everyone . . .*" Peter is asking us to love and respect our children. Then in Proverbs 22:6: "*Train a child in the way he should go, and when he is old he will not depart from it.*"

GODLY WAYS TO OVERCOME FAVORITISM IN CHILDREN AGED 1-11

God wants us as parents and grandparents to have the godly tools to use with our children. In reality, all children are favored by God and He, in effect, wants us to demonstrate the rotating favoritism as discussed above. Consequently, each child would receive a dose of favoritism to develop themselves and their self-confidence. Too much of a dose, like medicine, has very damaging effects on our children. The steps to avoid intentional favoritism are:

Accept the fact that you will inevitably show some favoritism to one or more of your children.

Listen to your children's complaints about intentional favoritism. They are very sensitive to it, so a complaint is probably revealing the truth.

Avoid discussing comparisons between your children with them or with others. You can make these comparisons privately and keep them to yourself. Comparisons between children are extremely divisive and rejecting leaving emotional scars on the lesser child. It is a poison that divides families and destroys the relationship between the parent and child. I will discuss this topic to a greater detail in the next chapter.

Avoid pitting your children in competition against each other. This situation creates a winner and a loser with the winner, appearing to the children, as receiving the parent's love and approval. Try to encourage and affirm all children in their achievements in their respective activities.

Avert judging children, which is an offshoot of competition. Children often ask a parent: "which one of us did _____ better," which is another way of initiating competition. In effect, the parent ends up taking sides. A better option is to encourage all children to try their best and give maximum effort. Use the rotating favoritism discussed above and tell your children, which one is the favorite this week. Next week it will be another child and keep the rotation going.

Developing loyalty between the children is an important antidote to favoritism. While most young children are by nature self-centered, instead teach them loyalty to each other and the family. This teaching can come from the parents modeling it through meeting the needs of others over their own. It shows unconditional love. I shall go into this topic in greater detail in the next chapter.

Never take sides in a fight between the children as you usually don't know the real reason for it. Also, it is so difficult to determine who started it so you run the risk of blaming the wrong child, creating anger. A better suggestion is to punish both parties.

Always try to tell your children that you love and appreciate them.

Look for a positive example to affirm each child. Such actions help build their confidence and help them to feel your love. These actions confirm what God does for us and demonstrates our following His principles.

These guidelines are designed particularly for young and middle aged kids. In the next chapter on teens to adults, we shall build on this list. We are seeking to diminish the causes of intentional favoritism and defeat any prospects of it developing. In effect, we want to eliminate the positions of favored one, unfavored one, or overlooked one and make everyone favored. All children strive to be loved and appreciated by their parents.

Summary:

1. Favoritism starts with the first child. Each partner adopts a role in child care with the mother usually the primary caretaker. Each parent devotes their attention with time, photos, and love for the child.

2. Physical appearance is a strong factor in deciding the favorite. Mothers often select the favored one. With no competition, the first child has the advantage of being favored.

3. Gender is second in selecting the favorite. Having the same gender as the parent creates strong ties because of mutual interests. The parent desires to leave a legacy with a similarly gendered child. In three children families with different sexes, gender usually decides the favorite. Parents may value the traits of their opposite-sexed children.

4. God wants parents to love all their children as a blessing from Him. Psalm 127:3. God gives each child their own abilities and He has a special plan for them. Psalm 40:5.

5. Several aspects of the child's development are:

a. Parent's greater attention to a new child, especially when a baby has difficulties. The first child doesn't understand that the new baby's needs and resents the attention shifting from him/her.

b. A first child's regression is a cry for attention, who doesn't understand what is going on with the new baby. The first child misses the former attention.

c. Parents ask the first child to help them with minor care of the new baby. Builds responsibility into the first child keeps them engaged.

6. The elements of favoritism to be aware of are:

a. Fluid favoritism—developed by Dr. Kent Ravenscroft gives every child an opportunity to be the favorite. Occurs with a child in the baby to toddler stages, but may occur later depending upon the parent's preference.

b. Sibling rivalry—where the children fight with each other for: the parent's attention, toys, food and who gets something first. It occurs in chaotic homes with competition. Favoritism for one child by a parent enhances sibling rivalry. When sibling rivalry is rampant, undermining each other becomes a goal.

c. Bonding—between children is a natural and desired step for reducing partiality. When children feel a personal closeness with each other from overcoming challenges or shared experiences. Parents enhance bonding when children watch their parent's positive interactions. Strong bonding between the children defeats favoritism. With bonding, favored children will often reject their special rewards from parents.

d. Intentional favoritism or dysfunctional favoritism—when a parent is devoted to one child and controls that child's performance for the parent's goals. A special bond develops between the parent and the favorite who receives constant benefits. Comparative favoritism is when the parent uplifts the abilities of the favorite over other children. God is against favoritism particularly intentional favoritism. Acts 10:34. He calls us to love and treat each child with respect. 1 John 4:7,

1 Peter 2:17 and Proverbs 22:6.

Godly Ways to Overcome Favoritism in Children Aged 1-11

1. God favors all children wants us to use rotating favoritism. Each child receives some favoritism, which develops self-confidence. Excessive partiality damages children. Steps to avoid intentional favoritism are:

a. Accept the fact that every parent will show some favoritism to one of your children.

b. Listen to your children's complaints about intentional favoritism. They are sensitive to it, so a complaint reveals the truth.

c. Avoid discussing comparisons between your children and others. Keep comparisons private. Comparisons are very rejecting, leaving emotional scars on the child. It divides families.

d. Avoid pitting your children in competition. It creates a winner and loser with the winner receiving the parent's love and approval. Encourage all children in their activities.

e. Avert judging children which is a form of competition. Children initiate competition causing the parent to take sides. Instead encourage all children to try their best.

f. Use rotating favoritism: one child is the favorite this week with another next week.

g. Never take sides in a fight as it is difficult to determine who started it. Suggest punishing both parties.

h. Always tell your children that you love and appreciate them. Look for a positive example to affirm each child. Such actions build their confidence and they feel your love. It confirms God's principles.

These guidelines are designed for young and middle aged kids to defeat intentional favoritism.

Discussion Questions

1. If you were the favorite in your family, how did it help you? How did it hurt you?

   Were you a first-born?

   Did you feel any guilt for your sibling over your position?

2. If you were a second or third child, how did you relate with your older sibling?

   Did you learn sibling loyalty in your family? How was your sibling rivalry?

3. As a parent do you or did you use rotating favoritism? Will you try it?

4. Where do you feel God is guiding you in your parenting? What changes are needed?

5. How have you been able to diminish any competition between your kids?

Chapter 7

Favoritism: Teenage Years into Adult Years

When Sally arrived in her home as a baby, her older sister Natalie was drawn to her and helped feed her. Natalie seemed fascinated by her younger sister and played with her. Soon, a bond began to form with these positive daily interactions. Even though there was a two and a half year age difference between them, yet they related closely. Their parents encouraged them to play cooperatively together. Her mother would say, "Don't the two of you play so well together. You hardly ever fight." While there were isolated incidents of sibling rivalry, but none was serious. They enjoyed discussing their experiences in school.

As they both became teenagers, their sibling loyalty became so strong that they trusted each other by sharing their personal secrets and closest feelings. Thus an intimate bond had been formed built on their positive experiences and interactions. Natalie would help Sally with suggestions on how to get along with the other girls and even the boys. One day in high school, two senior girls started picking on Sally, who was only a freshmen. Natalie saw Sally crying from the harsh verbal attack. Immediately she rushed to her sister's aid, stopping the aggressive girls and comforting her sister. Sally felt so relieved and grateful to Natalie for being there for her in this terrible crisis. This incident forged in Sally's mind a lasting memory of trust in her sister.

The two sisters kept in regular contact by telephone and email maintaining the tight relationship. They visited each other even when Sally moved away to Florida. Birthdays and anniversaries were celebrated by each sister. Then Natalie got very sick and appeared to be dying. Sally rushed to Natalie's side, ministering to her needs and praying for her recovery for several weeks. Sadly, Natalie died in Sally's loving arms. Sally felt crushed, but realized that they both had a very unique relationship of sibling loyalty for most of her life with her dear sibling.

We see in this story how sibling loyalty develops, becomes intimate, and can develop the power to last a lifetime. Our siblings know us, both warts and good points, but with strong loyalty we will be there for each other when a crisis comes.

The teenage years, considered by most experts as 12 to 18 years old, are a time of great upheaval in the child and the dynamics of the family. Great physical, emotional, and even spiritual changes occur. Adjusting to these rapid changes in height, voice, and sexuality bring increased stress into the teen's life and thereby into the family. The teen's emotions seem to fluctuate wildly. I can still remember my father calling my teenaged sister "storm and stress" from her dramatic emotional swings.

The teen begins searching for their identity as an adult man or woman, departing from their role as a child. Linda Sonna PhD, in her book corroborates this point: "They are trying to become independent. To do that, they must emerge from the shadow of parents and older siblings so that they can carve out a separate identity." God is directing these changes to help develop the maturity of the teen. Teens have a heightened sensitivity to any existing parental favoritism and are not afraid to voice their strong feelings against the unfairness of it. They resent their position as unfavored, or overlooked ones. Basically, they are telling their parents that they aren't dealing with a submissive child anymore.

Their rebellion against the status-quo disturbs the previous harmony in the family, thereby incurring the wrath and disdain of their parents. Thus, a rebellious favorite child may lose their status unless the parent, displaying intentional favoritism with the child, maintains their firm control of that teen. Despite their rebellious nature, they still seek parental affirmation for their actions and new ideas. This is a time when teens tend to push and even break through boundaries that the parents and society set. They desire to explore new places, new ideas and even dangerous things like trying drugs, alcohol, sex, and fast driving. Teens seem bent on experiencing these things for themselves, often rejecting the warnings from adults of their danger. They like the idea of being in control of their lives and making their own decisions about these dangers. Regrettably, too many succumb to the drugs and get hooked. I see them come into Syracuse Teen Challenge every day some from many good, caring families, but these teens have been headstrong in pursuing their own way. Their destructive actions have disrupted the family's harmony causing many teens become rejected by their families.

Joshua came to Teen Challenge searching for help with his meth addiction. In reality, Josh had experienced a life of pain. His mother died when he was two years old so he never knew her. Both he and his brother, Larry, were given up to a foster family. So he doesn't remember seeing his father for long periods. At the same time, his five year old brother started beating Josh up to enforce his will on him. These regular beatings would continue unabated until he was 12 when Josh fought back.

At seven, Josh was sexually abused by one of the relatives and this abuse continued for two more years. Ironically, Larry was also abused by the same person, but at 11 Larry told his parents and it stopped for both of them. This experience drew the brothers closer together for a short time. However, with the chaos in their family, his brother started beating him again for another three years. Josh was introduced to meth by a friend and, as he told me, "I felt peace in my life for the first time. It seemed to release all the pain in my life." Meth soon became a god for him as he would do anything to get the money for it.

At Syracuse Teen Challenge, I introduced Josh to Theophastic Prayer where he relayed his story of anguish. Fortunately, Jesus brought him the real peace that he had always sought, but had never really found.

In this true story, we see the damage of sibling rivalry and why it is so prevalent in families living in chaos. We see the destruction of a sibling relationship and of damaged lives. Both siblings were not aware of the benefits of sibling loyalty, which could have strengthened them both in the face of such adversities.

Teens push for greater privileges at home like: later bed times, learning to drive a car, and having a cell phone. Many teens, however, want the adult privileges without accepting the necessary responsibilities and requirements to earn them like: maintaining reasonable grades in school, handling chores competently, and trying their best in school and activities. My wife and I found it necessary to write out a contract with our teenage son. In it we set forth that we provided him with food, clothing, shelter and love. He earned the privileges of: TV, use of the car, and telephone (this was before cell phones), by earning at least a C in his high school courses, doing his chores correctly, being respectful, and avoiding certain negative friends and drugs. We found that the contract worked effectively when we enforced its penalties by restricting his privileges when he had violated the contract.

In the teenage years and later as adults we encounter different important challenges, In addition, there are several important principles, as I mentioned in the previous chapter, that are very helpful in the process of reducing intentional favoritism and its effects. These are:

Sibling loyalty. It is when children commit to support the other sibling especially when that sibling is under stress or being hurt in some manner. Children learn this principle from their parents, older siblings and extended family modeling it to them. Siblings develop a faithful allegiance to each other because of their mutual love. The godly concept of sacrificing self-interest for the sake of another person is found in Philippians 2:3-4: *"Do nothing out of selfish ambition or vain conceit but in humility consider others as better than yourself. Each of you should look not only to your own interests, but also the interests of others"* Such selflessness binds siblings together so that they think and care for each other. Carol Kuykendall in her book, *Five-Star Families*, explains: "Children learn loyalty from what they see: support and kindness for each other. Stepping over our own needs to meet the needs of others in the family. We hope they learn to love others well because they have been well loved."

Loyalty is a choice requiring support whether it is verbal or actions. The child learns to feel empathy for the other sibling by coming to their aid when they are hurting or defending them against attack. Jane Isay spotlights this point in her book, *Mom Likes You Best*, when she states: "What makes these different from the other relationships? The answer seems to be connection, a deep and powerful empathy and mutual respect. Brothers and sisters who enjoy this connection confide in each other with confidence, laugh at themselves and each other, and celebrate their relaxed intimacy." Many times competitive siblings in the home who, even dislike each other, will fly to the defense of the other when they see them attacked at home, school, or even church. Each experience of support builds a stronger bond between the siblings so that when a crisis comes they are there for each other. Such situations occur frequently at end of life crises.

Solomon in Ecclesiastes 4:9-12 speaks to such a bond built by sibling loyalty: *"Two are better than one because they have a good return for their work: If one falls down, his friend* (also a sibling). *But pity the man that falls and has no one to help him up! Also if two lie down together, they will keep warm. But how can one keep warm alone? Though one may be overpowered, two can defend themselves. A cord of three strands is not quickly broken."* These verses reflect how God wants us to develop sibling loyalty for the strong support it brings to all siblings in time of need. In the last verse, the third strand is God supporting the other two and making the cord (bond) between them unbreakable.

Strong sibling loyalty severely reduces sibling rivalry and the effects of intentional favoritism in the following examples: favorites have been known to ask their parents to give their rewards to the other sibling(s). Also, favorites, because of their empathy developed through sibling loyalty often feel guilty for their sibling(s) over their favored status. As a result, favorites often regret that they were ever selected as the favored one.

Teaching children the value of sibling cooperation vs. sibling competition. Some parents believe that fostering competition between siblings makes them become stronger to enable them to handle the challenges of life. Joseph Kennedy, father of President John F. Kennedy, believed in this concept by fostering never ending competitions between his many sons to develop their ability to compete in the political world. Siblings naturally learn to become competitive from adults and other teens in school. There are, however, positive influences such as coaches that teach cooperating and working together as a team member when competing.

Aggressive sibling competitions can lead to distrust developing between the siblings. Competitive family environments focus the individual on winning the prize and encouraging the sibling to use any means possible to win. Such an environment, often promotes breaking the rules of the family, society, and God, which can destroy the person's achievements. Linda Sonna speaks to this condition in her book, *The Everything Parent's Guide To Raising Siblings:* "Beating or one-upping a sibling provides a temporary emotional boast, but it doesn't last. They may turn every situation into a competition in an effort to garner the continuing affirmations they need to feel good about themselves." Additionally, competitive siblings look on their other siblings as rivals and are motivated to undermine them. These attitudes create lack of trust between siblings, which may destroy their relationship. Thus, sibling competition only enflames sibling rivalry, especially when intentional favoritism is being employed by a parent.

This competition is the opposite of God's plan for us as Jesus tells us in Matthew 19:19 to: "*'. . . love your neighbor as yourself.'*" God wants us to help our sibling and cooperate together. By working cooperatively, we accomplish far more and, at the same time, gain more personal satisfaction for us and for others.

Jealousy. Teenagers find that jealousy is a powerful force on them as they endeavor to connect with their peers as they break away from their parents. Teens make comparisons with each other over abilities, achievements, and looks resulting in winners and losers. Cliques are formed that include only the winners while losers are excluded. This situation has such power on teenagers who strive to be accepted for who they are with their own abilities and skills.

I can painfully remember the fact that I was not skilled enough or good looking enough to become a part of the clique in my High School. Being shy, my social skills were limited. The feeling of being unaccepted hurt so much when I was trying to break away from being under control of my parents. Feeling so depressed, I would come home and escape into reading books and television. There, I could live in a different world and feel accepted. Going to school was such a struggle with its daily dose of rejection. In reality, I had become jealous of those in the clique.

After going to college, I realized that I had abilities that I had not explored in high school. Encouraged by a teacher, I tried out for a part in a play for the first time in my life and got a minor part. While I wasn't ever a leading man, I did secure some good minor roles. Another was speaking to groups. Having a deep fear of speaking in front of groups, it took real courage to face my fear. Finally, I decided to do it and ended up speaking to over to 20 different groups in one year. Success in these new ventures created a new confidence in myself and my new abilities. Regrettably, it was much later that I found the Lord and gained the great confidence He brought into my life. I found that I had value and worth as a child of God as I learned that: "... *The Lord does not look at the things man looks at. Man looks at the outward appearance, but the Lord looks at the heart.*" 1 Samuel 16:7.

Jealousy is really wanting to be like another person who you think is better in some skill, looks, talent, or social status. God made us all unique so that we have to search to find our true skills. Oftentimes our fear of failure holds us back from even trying new opportunities. Ask God to help you find your talents that He has placed in you. You will be surprised.

Teaching children family-centered values. Means teaching your children that maintaining the harmony and well-being of the family is a paramount value for everyone in the family. Also, siblings are taught to help both financially and physically with the needs of parents and hurting siblings. The quality of their inter-relationships between siblings and their parents is the most important value compared to winning achievements or gaining greater material possessions. To reward their children, parents will give them extra attention instead of a trinket. Also, older children are given additional responsibilities like caring for the younger children, but are given extra privileges. Developing and strengthening those family relationships is modeled and stressed by the parents with their children so that it becomes ingrained in their children's psyche.

Often coming from lower economic means, the family promotes family cooperation, which is often vital for the family's survival living in harsh physical conditions. Sibling competition is downplayed so that sibling rivalry is diminished. Such family unity can build strong sibling relationships at the cost of subverting the individual child's achievements and goals. Family-centered values are taught frequently in families from Spanish and Asian cultures. Spanish students at Syracuse Teen Challenge, however, have told me how some family members will abuse the system by not working, yet expect other siblings to support them. Also, intelligent children may be asked to relinquish their future goals to financially support the family. Nonetheless, many family experts are recommending that more American families utilize cooperation versus competition to promote greater family harmony.

On the other hand, our individualistic North American society offers the opposite value by promoting individual sibling thought and achievement. The parents encourage their children to succeed in competition with others and allow sibling rivalry to exist in the family. Siblings are strongly encouraged to develop their education or skills to achieve financial success, which reflects favorably on the parents. The focus of this value is on the future achievements versus the present focus of the family-values method where parents give each child more specialized attention. In the individualistic family, the parents don't want their children to give up their goals for the family. For example, toys or an allowance are often given the child as rewards. Of course sacrificing for the family can be abused and even violates U.S. laws, especially if a child is taken out of school excessively.

Below are some additional ways for parents of teenagers to avoid intentional favoritism in teenage and adult children. They augment the list of suggestions for young children.

Don't ask teenagers to set an example. Expecting a teenager to be an example for younger siblings is often ineffective. Teenagers usually want to live their own lives separating themselves from their younger siblings. Instead parents should directly address the teenager to correct their language or actions instead of forcing them to be an example.

Avoid taking sides in a fight. When a fight occurs between teenagers, parents feel obligated to step in to stop it. Parents too often see the fight after it started so they miss who started the fight. They see the aggressor and take action against that teen often letting the provoker off with little or no discipline. Instead, it is better to punish both parties for not working it out or cooperating together. At Syracuse Teen Challenge, we often punish the whole student body for some offenses. In that way, the students deal with the real offenders and usually the offending action stops. This action is a way of emphasizing the teenagers working conflicts out without fighting.

ADULT FAVORITISM

"I have been afflicted with favoritism most of my life!" exclaimed Roger, an African-American in his mid thirties. I had known Roger several years ago when he came to Syracuse Teen Challenge for help with a drug addiction. As his mentor, we developed a friendship that continued after he left Teen Challenge. Roger painfully recounted how he had been the unfavored one in his family from an early age. His older brother, Sam, was highly favored by both his parents. Roger went on how, "Sam was so adored by my parents even when he beat me up, which was almost every week. I felt so abused and left out."

The more Roger talked you could feel the agony of being unfavored by his parents had to the point affected him even as an adult. Sam, it seemed, was never disciplined for his attacks on his brother. Roger learned to hate his brother into his adult years when he started using drugs to medicate his pain. During those depressing days in Roger's life, serious thoughts of suicide went through his mind Then he discovered Jesus and he realized his need to forgive his brother. When Sam got into trouble and went to jail, Roger visited and forgave him. This Christian act freed them both and they became close friends.

This story demonstrates how intentional favoritism, initiated in childhood, can start to destroy a life and its effects can carry over into adult years. Some people have told me that favoritism in childhood diminishes as the child grows up, but as this true story demonstrates, this concept is a myth. Adults often carry the anguish of being unfavored for the rest of their lives and can easily end up becoming depressed, bitter old people. Yet we see in this story how a relationship with God can dramatically change a life and build a new connection with an alienated sibling.

Some of the characteristics of adult favoritism are:

Continuing depression. A study entitled, "Mother's Differentiation and Depressive Symptoms among Adult Children" in the April 10, 2010 *"Journal of Marriage"* found adult children that had been unfavored by their mothers experienced depression into middle age. This depression can lead to thoughts of suicide as in our story. Also, the lives of these adults were repeatedly afflicted by the ups and downs from chronic depression.

Lack of self-esteem. Since they were measured by their parent(s) against another sibling and found lacking, their self-worth is weak. These adults struggle to find their worth and place in life. Lacking God in their life, they measure themselves by what others say of them. Thus, seeking the approval of others, they tend to become people-pleasers that end up pleasing no one. I have found this situation true at Syracuse Teen Challenge where students into their thirties and forties face this same struggle.

Medicate their pain with alcohol or drugs. Unable to find relief from their anguish, they too often seek a quick fix from drugs and/or alcohol. While these may provide a temporary relief, their side effects trap them into a terrible dependency that gradually destroys their life.

Adults recall their damaged emotions. Unfavored adults struggle with powerful feelings in their older years as they have been relayed to me by many older hurting adults. These include questions regarding: why they were abandoned by the favoring parent(s), pondering what they may have done wrong to deserve this pain, feelings of not being appreciated, frequent sadness, isolation, and anxiety. These adults live in an emotional prison controlled by their painful memories.

The urgency to turn to God. David tells us in Psalm 34:18: *"The Lord is close to the brokenhearted and saves those who are crushed in spirit."* The Lord wants to help heal our broken heart and our spirit crushed by intentional favoritism. The Bible is clear that intentional favoritism is a sin, as James 2:9 states: *"But if you show favoritism, you sin and are convicted by the law as lawbreakers."* Consequently, we need Jesus to help heal us from this deadly sin. If we will just draw close to Jesus, he wants to give us a new positive direction and strength to overcome the damage caused by ungodly favoritism.

In addition, He gives us hope that we can discover a brighter future by following Him. When we are depressed we have lost hope, but He will give us a new and eternal hope. David in Psalm 62:5-6 exemplifies this: *"Find rest, O my soul, in God alone; my hope comes from him. He alone is my rock and my salvation; he is my fortress, I will not be shaken."* When we are devoted to Jesus we have an eternal hope through our resurrection from this earth into heaven. Then the things of this world will be viewed as temporary, while we seek the eternal significance of living with Jesus in our daily lives.

Adult sibling rivalry. Many people mistakenly think that negative sibling rivalry ends in the teenage years, but frequently it continues into adulthood as studies show that up to 45% of adult siblings suffer from continuing sibling strife. Jeanne Safer in her book, *Cain's Legacy,* points out: ". . . the majority of adult siblings, when questioned late in life, confess that they feel worse about unresolved relationships with brothers and sisters than about other unfinished business." We see that negative sibling rivalry started in childhood presents even greater anguish in adulthood. Parents need to use the following steps to limit and hopefully resolve it for their adult children:

Don't take sides. Offer advice and suggestions on how to resolve issues using godly wisdom. Emphasize that you don't want to be forced into their conflict. Provide a listening ear to both sides as James speaks in verse 1:19: "*. . . Everyone should be quick to listen, slow to speak and slow to become angry.*" Remember to listen not only to the words, but the emotions behind the words that probably reveal their true intentions.

Discuss with them about how their rivalry affects the family. Gather the family and discuss the negative effects that the rivalry is having on all the family members. Provide suggestions, including topics that are off limits so as to limit the number of clashes between the siblings. I have seen this solution used in my own family where we agreed to not discuss politics and we found better family harmony. The siblings agree not to discuss topics where they disagree.

Keep away from comparisons. I mentioned this earlier, but it is also very relevant to adults. Comparing success in careers, families, and abilities is very destructive to family peace. Adult children still seek to please their parents and are more sensitive to comparisons. The goal should be to value each adult for their own distinct achievements and abilities without being compared to their sibling.

Help them to take time to understand each other. Everyone wants to be understood for who they are and their values. To truly understand someone requires spending extensive time together relating on a personal level. This principle to be understood is a strong desire in everyone and is critical for people wanting to deeply connect with each other.

Suggest the siblings meet weekly at a neutral location. This suggestion gives the siblings and opportunity to develop a better relationship in a public place. There they would be constrained from using violence and/or harsh words with each other. Meeting regularly allows them the opportunity to work through issues together and provides positive life experiences together.

Provide senior wisdom or direction. Because of our life experiences, we, as parents, have learned positive ways of coping with life's challenges. We can use this wisdom to help other adults through trials, as I am doing with Roger and in my weekly mentoring sessions at Syracuse Teen Challenge. My guide is the Lord and what His direction is for Roger's life and my mentee. Proverbs 3:5-6: "*Trust in the Lord with all your heart and lean not on your own understanding; in all your ways acknowledge him, and he will make your paths straight.*"

Some differences that occur in adult favoritism versus child or teenage favoritism: Unfortunately, parents more frequently exhibit favoritism to those adult children that:

1. Live closer to them. This proximity allows for more frequent meetings and reinforces the relationship.

2. Provide the most emotional or financial support to the parents. Such support connects with the parents creating a stronger bond.

3. Are daughters as they are usually more dependent upon their parents. Thus their daughters do not completely "leave and cleave" to their new husbands.

4. Share the values of the parents, particularly faith in Jesus Christ. Having come to Jesus through a parent or later from someone else creates a strong connection. Ironically, I have on occasion felt closer to a Christian brother or sister than an unbelieving blood relative. Jesus affirms this in Mathew 12:46-50: "*While Jesus was still talking to the crowd, his mother and brothers stood outside, wanting to speak to him. Someone told him, 'Your mother and brothers are standing outside, wanting to speak to you.'*

He replied to him, 'Who is my mother, and who are my brothers?' Pointing to his disciples, he said, 'Here are my mother and my brothers. For whoever does the will of my Father in heaven is my brother and sister and mother.'"

The adult, wounded by intentional favoritism often suffers more from its consequences than when they were a child or were a teenager. Regrettably, adults too often have buried their pain in denial, trying to get rid of it. Such inaction can lead to starting dangerous generational favoritism. Resolution of this sin can be overcome with frank discussions of its severe effects on you with your parents and other siblings to help them find God's forgiveness. Most unfavored siblings tend to take out their frustration and anger on the favored sibling neglecting to address their parents for their part in the situation. After all, it was the parent(s) that initiated the intentional favoritism.

As a paradox, parents frequently live in denial, not wanting to admit their role in their partiality. They want to be thought of as "good parents" by all their children. Consequently, often a paralysis of denial exists between the children and parents since no one wants to admit any responsibility.

Summary:

1. The teenager's physical, emotional, and spiritual changes create stress on the teen and family. The teen's emotions fluctuate wildly. Teens depart search for their identity as adults.

2. Teens sense intentional favoritism and voice strong feelings against it. They resent being unfavored or overlooked ones. Their rebellion disturbs the family harmony. A rebellious favorite child may lose their status unless the parent controls the teen using intentional favoritism.

3. Teens tend to break boundaries. They try experiencing new places, ideas and dangerous things. They want to be in control of their lives and make their own decisions.

a. Teens want greater privileges. They seek adult privileges without accepting the responsibilities to earn them.

4. Several important principles to reduce intentional favoritism in teens are:

a. Sibling loyalty. Children commit to support their sibling when he/she is under stress. Children learn this principle from the modeling of parents, older siblings, and extended family. Siblings develop a faithful allegiance to each other because of their mutual care. This godly concept is sacrificing self for another person. Philippians 2:3-4. Loyalty is a choice requiring support. The teen feels empathy for their sibling by helping them when they are hurting. Even competitive siblings defend the other when they are attacked. Each experience of support builds a stronger bond. Ecclesiastes 4:9-12. God wants us to develop sibling loyalty. Examples of sibling loyalty are when favorites: give their rewards to the other sibling(s), feel guilty for their favored status, and regret that they were favored.

b. Teaching the value of sibling cooperation vs. sibling competition. Some parents believe that sibling competition makes them stronger. Siblings learn to competitive from adults and other teens. Positive influences are coaches. Aggressive sibling competition leads to distrust between siblings. Competitive families focus on the teen winning by any means. Such action promotes breaking the rules of the family, society and God.

Competitive siblings undermine their other siblings creating a lack of trust and destroying their relationship. Sibling competition enflames sibling rivalry. This competition is the opposite of God's plan. Matthew 19:19. God wants us to help our sibling and cooperate together. We accomplish more by working cooperatively and gain personal satisfaction.

c. Jealousy. Teenagers find jealousy can be a powerful force in their lives. Teens make comparisons over abilities, achievements, and looks resulting in winners and losers. Winners form cliques that exclude los-

ers. The teen craves the skill, looks or talent of the winning teens. Ask
God to help you find joy in your unique talents.

d. Teaching children family-centered values. Teach your children that
family harmony is a paramount value. Siblings are taught to help
financially and physically meet the needs of parents and hurting siblings. The quality of inter-relationships between siblings and parents is
more important than more possessions. Parents reward teens with
extra attention instead of a toy. Teens are given responsibilities as caring for the younger children, but get extra privileges.

Sibling competition is downplayed. Family unity builds sibling relationships but subverts the individual's achievements. Some siblings
abuse the system by not working, yet expect siblings to support them.
Capable children relinquish their goals to financially support the family. Family experts recommend American families adopt this concept.

North American society values individual thought and achievement. Parents encourage their children to succeed in competition and
allow sibling rivalry. Siblings are expected to get education to achieve
financial success. The focus is on the future versus the present condition of the family-centered values. U.S. laws limit the children's ability
to sacrifice for the family.

Ways for parents to avoid intentional favoritism in teenagers and adult
children are:

Don't ask teenagers to set an example. Teenagers want to live separate
from their younger siblings. Instead parents should correct the language or actions of their teenager.

Avoid taking sides in a fight. Parents feel obligated to stop it. They
punish the last aggressor, but allow the provoker off. Instead, punish
both parties for not working it out.

Adults carry the anguish of being unfavored into old age becoming depressed, bitter people. A daily relationship with God can dramatically change that. Some characteristics of adult favoritism are:

Continuing depression. A study in the *"Journal of Marriage"* found unfavored adults experienced depression leading to thoughts of suicide.

Lack of self-esteem. These adults struggle to find their true worth and depend upon what others say of them. They tend to become people-pleasers ending up pleasing no one.

Medicate their pain with alcohol or drugs. Seeking quick relief from their pain, they turn to drugs and/or alcohol. They provide a temporary fix, but create a dependency.

Adults recall their damaged emotions. The powerful feelings of unfavored adults include: abandonment, trying to understand what they did wrong, feeling unappreciated, frequent sadness, isolation, and anxiety. These adults live in an emotional prison.

The urgency to turn to God. Psalm 34:18. The Lord wants to heal our broken heart crushed by intentional favoritism. He treats favoritism as a sin. James 2:9. We need Jesus to heal us from this sin, give us a new positive direction, and give us hope to overcome our depression. Psalm 62:5-6. Jesus gives us an eternal hope through His resurrection We thereby find our eternal significance.

Adult sibling rivalry. Frequently continues into adulthood. Such rivalry starts in childhood continues into adulthood. Parents use the following steps to limit it:

Don't take sides. Offer suggestions on how to resolve issues using godly wisdom. Don't be forced into their conflict. Provide a listening ear to both sides. James 1:19. Remember to listen to the emotions behind the words. They reveal the true intentions.

Discuss with them about how their rivalry affects the family. Discuss with the siblings the negative effects of their rivalry on the family. Suggest topics that are off limits. Siblings can agree to disagree.

Keep away from comparisons. Comparing success in careers, families, and abilities is destructive to family peace. Value each adult for their own achievements and abilities.

Help them to take time to understand each other. Take the time needed to understand your sibling for their thoughts and values. Remember, everyone wants to be understood.

Suggest the siblings meet weekly at a neutral location. It allows siblings to build better relationships. Meeting regularly gives them the opportunity to work through issues.

Provide senior wisdom or direction. Senior parents have learned positive ways of coping and can provide valuable wisdom for their adult siblings. Proverbs 3:5-6.

Intentional favoritism wounds adults more than a child or teenager as adults bury their pain in denial. Resolution is discussing its effects with parents and other siblings. Unfavored siblings take out their frustration on favored siblings; neglecting to blame their parents for initiating the intentional favoritism.

Discussion Questions

1. As a teenager, did you confront your parents on why they treated you as an unfavored or overlooked child?

   Did you rebel against their treatment of you?

2. Was your relationship with your sibling controlled by loyalty or rivalry?

   What did you wish it could be today?

3. Was your sibling relationship mainly cooperative or competitive?

   How does that make you feel?

4. Did you teach your children family values?

   Are you teaching them to your grandkids?

5. Of the six characteristics of adult children, which ones have affected you the most?

   What have you done to handle them in your life?

Chapter 8
Favoritism in the Bible

God condemns favoritism in the Bible starting with Leviticus 19:15: *Do not pervert justice; do not show partiality to the poor or favoritism to the great, but judge your neighbor fairly."* This theme of denouncing favoritism is echoed in Exodus 6:7, Proverbs 24:23, and Malachi 2:9. It continues into the New Testament in Romans 2:11: *"For God does not show favoritism"* and continuing in Colossians 3:25, and James 2:3-9. Yet, we have examples of partiality found in many godly families in the Bible. Why is it that such a strong command is disregarded by God's people? The reason is that we see men and women exercising their free will to strongly prefer certain people because of similar interests, personalities, or even appearances. What can we learn to watch for or to avoid in our lives from these biblical life stories of intentional favoritism and sibling rivalry?

The story of hostile sibling rivalry: Cain and Abel.
Genesis 4:2-10

Starting in Genesis 4 we encounter the earliest example of sibling strife between Abel and his brother Cain. Both are asked to present an offering to God. Abel brings the firstborn from his flock as a sacrifice, while Cain brings his fruits from the soil. Abel's sacrifice is accepted by God, but Cain's is rejected. Cain then feeling the intense pain of the rejection, decides to end the competition by killing his brother and hides from the crime. Secular commentators like Jeanne Safer psychologist propose in her book, *Cain's Legacy,* that God favored Abel, which is why Cain was so angry. She blames God for lack of fairness with Cain: "He (God) abdicates His own responsibility for turning Cain against Abel and adds insult to injury by blaming the victim/aggressor for failing to acknowledge that Cain has any reason to be angry in the first place . . ." Such a human approach fails to consider God's requirements for the sacrifice that were not met by Cain and He also knew the true character of Cain. Many Bible scholars and commentators have also questioned why God rejected Cain's sacrifice. While the Bible is not totally clear on the exact basis, biblical scholars respond that the answer seems to lie in several plausible reasons:

1. Cain's negative attitude when he gave his sacrifice. Hebrews 11:4 addresses this point: *"By faith Abel offered God a better sacrifice than Cain did. By faith he was commended as a righteous man, when God spoke well of his offerings. And by faith still speaks, even though he is dead."* Also, Henry M. Morris confirms this point in his book, *The Genesis Record: A scientific & devotional commentary on the book of beginnings:* "At any rate, his heart was not right before the Lord, and his offering was not in faith as his brother's. Therefore, God rejected his gift." We need to have a humble and contrite attitude when giving to God, which is more important than the gift itself. In addition, Abel offered his sacrifice in faith implying a connection to God.

The Apostle John in 1 John 3:11-12 speaks of Cain's heart condition: *"We should love one another, not as Cain who was of the wicked one and murdered his brother. And why did he murder him? Because his works were evil and his brother's righteous."* Then again in Jude 11, we read, *"They have taken the way of Cain,"* referring to lawless men. This possibly could mean that they, like Cain, had their own ways of disobedient worship instead of by faith. We too may have hatred lurking in our lives, especially against our sibling, God knows of it and wants to help us overcome it. He is looking for us to confess any hatred towards our sibling(s) so we can receive His forgiveness and love.

2. The wrong sacrifice. Under the rules for sacrifices acceptable to God in Leviticus 17:11, God asks for a blood sacrifice: *"For the life of a creature is in the blood, and I have given it to you to make atonement for yourselves on the altar; it is the blood that makes atonement for one's life."*

Abel gave a blood sacrifice while Cain did not. Perhaps Cain didn't know better, but God sacrificed blood when He killed the animals to cloth his parents, Adam and Eve, after they had eaten of the forbidden fruit (Genesis 3:21). Furthermore, we read in Genesis 3:17: *"To Adam he said, 'Because you have listened to your wife and ate from the tree about which I commanded you, 'You must not eat of it.' Cursed is the ground because of you . . .'"* As we see in this verse God is cursing the ground so perhaps God didn't want any sacrifice to come from the ground.

3. The quality of Cain's offering. Genesis 4:4 states: *"But Abel brought fat portions from some of the firstborn of his flock."* The key point is that Abel brought his firstborn, which implies that Abel had been given instructions by someone of what to offer. In addition, the firstborn is considered the highest quality. Meanwhile, there is no description of Cain's offering, which seems strange. In Genesis 4:6: *"Then the Lord said to Cain, 'Why are you angry? Why is your face downcast? If you do what is right, will you not be accepted? . . . .'"*. This verse strongly implies that they both had been instructed on the right type and quality of the sacrifice to bring.

In summary, it appears that Cain's sacrifice was rejected by God because of his attitude and, possibly, also because of the type and quality of his sacrifice. Cain seemed to have a hostile attitude toward his sacrifice, which God discerned. Even though God rejected Cain's offering, God gives him another opportunity to sacrifice correctly, but warns him of the danger in his heart in Genesis 4:6-7: *"Then the Lord said to Cain, 'Why are you angry? Why is your face downcast? If you do what is right, will you not be accepted? But if you do not what is right, sin is crouching at your door; it desires to have you, but you must master it.'"* Cain fails to master that sin so, instead of following God's advice; he murders his competition, his brother Abel.

Lesson for us. We too need to develop a heart like Able that is humble and obedient. Too often we can be like Cain with hatred in our hearts when we give and/or worship God. Oh Lord, help cleanse our hearts of any bitterness and unforgiveness so that we can give and truly worship you with a pure heart.

The story of dual favoritism: Jacob and Esau.
Genesis 25:24-34, 27:1-41, & 28-33:7

Isaac married Rebekah and she became pregnant with twins that fought each other in her womb. The Lord told her that she had two nations within her and that the older (Esau) would serve the younger (Jacob). The boys grew up with Esau becoming an able hunter with a desire for eating wild game, while Jacob preferred staying home and cooking. Physically, Esau's skin was a hairy and had a strong body, while Jacob's skin was smooth. Esau had an impetuous nature that would yield to his appetites, while Jacob was quiet and a conniver. Esau's interests and abilities appealed to his father who favored him, while Rebekah favored Jacob for his qualities. Thus, we had dual intentional favoritism in the family that led to strife.

One day Esau came home famished and craved the stew that Jacob was cooking. Seizing his opportunity, Jacob bargained the stew for Esau's birthright. The birthright entitled the firstborn to a double inheritance and leadership of the family. Later, Rebekah heard her almost blind husband telling Esau to make him a meal of fresh game then he will give Esau his blessing. The father's blessing was significant because it bound the birthright to that son and could not be reversed. Ignoring God's promise for Jacob, Rebekah focused her intentional favoritism on getting Jacob her husband's blessing. In Genesis 27:9, Rebekah tells Jacob: *"'Go out to the flock and bring me two choice young goats, so I can prepare some tasty food for your father, just the way he likes it. Then take it to your father to eat, so that he can give you his blessing before he dies.'"* She also dressed Jacob in animal skins to simulate Esau's skin. The scheme worked and Isaac mistakenly gave his blessing to Jacob denying Esau his rightful benefit.

This evil plot, hatched by intentional favoritism, unleashes the following consequences for the family and even Israel.

Rebakah never sees Jacob again as Jacob is forced to flee from Esau's wrath over the evil plot that was done to him.

Later Jacob is very worried that his brother will kill him when they meet again for the first time.

The family is torn about by dissension as Jacob left for a long time.

Jacob is later deceived himself by his uncle Laban who tricks him into marrying the older sister and not the one Jacob loved.

Esau formed the nation of Edom, which later was a constant thorn to the country of Israel with wars and constant attacks.

Thus, we see the serious unintended consequences of intentional favoritism on everyone in the family and Israel itself. When the two brothers meet again 20 years later, they have both become successful. Esau has forgiven his brother's deceitfulness and doesn't harbor any revenge. Genesis 33:4 relays the rest of the story: *"But Esau ran to meet Jacob and embraced him; he threw his arms around his neck and kissed him. And they wept."* Esau had released his previous bitterness, thereby enabling him to be restored with his brother. The pain of intentional favoritism had been broken. While Esau seeks reconciliation, Jacob is still so distrusting that reconciliation is beyond him.

Lesson for us. We too need to try to grant forgiveness when our sibling has wronged us. This story shows us the power of forgiveness to remove the poison of resentment for our sibling in our hearts. Through forgiveness, we find restoration and possible reconciliation with our sibling, which brings peace in our lives.

The story of favoritism and hostile sibling rivalry: Joseph and his brothers. Genesis 37, 39-45:17.

Joseph was the oldest child of Jacob's favorite wife, Rachel. When he was born he had six older brothers from Jacob's other wife, Leah, plus two other older brothers from Leah's maid servant. The family's sibling rivalry, which started with Jacob and his brother Esau, continued with Jacob's two wives who in turn passed it onto their respective sons. There can be such a strong tendency for adults to repeat favoritism and hostile sibling rivalry that happened to them as children. As we discussed earlier, our brains become wired to repeat these painful actions committed upon us later on our children.

Thus we see Jacob, now renamed Israel by God, favoring Joseph in Genesis 37:3-4 *"Now Israel loved Joseph more than any of his other sons, because he had been born to him in his old age; and he made a richly ornamented robe for him. When his brothers saw that their father loved him more than any of them, they hated him and could not speak a kind word to him."* The father's blatant favoritism results in sibling hatred for his favorite son.

Joseph flaunts his favorite position by wearing Israel's robe out to see his brothers. This insensitive action arouses his siblings' envy who develop a murderous plot to kill him. However, they feel guilty as revealed in Genesis 37:27: *"'. . . he is our own brother, our own flesh and blood.'"* They throw him into a cistern in the meantime. Upon seeing a merchant caravan headed for Egypt, they sell Joseph to them expecting that Joseph will die in Egypt. To complete their deception, the brothers slaughter a goat, dip Joseph's robe in the blood, and present it to their father saying Joseph was killed by an animal. Israel, a deceiver himself, is deceived again and grieves his son's death.

In Egypt Joseph is sold to Potiphar, Pharaoh's captain of the guard, and does so well that he is put in charge of the household. Potiphar's wife tries unsuccessfully to lure Joseph into her bedroom and Joseph is jailed because of her false accusation. Joseph is humbled in jail, but God is with him enabling him to correctly interpret the dreams of two of Pharaoh's servants. Years later, when Pharaoh has two dreams that no one in court can interpret, the servant who was in jail with Joseph, mentions Joseph's ability. Quickly he is brought to Pharaoh and with God's help Joseph accurately interprets the dreams. The region will experience seven years of prosperous crops then seven years of drought. Joseph is put in charge of managing all crops in Egypt and prepares for the coming devastation. All of this is God's plan to save many people including Israel's family and to ultimately restore Joseph's relationship with his brothers. With the advent of the drought, Joseph's brothers come to Egypt to buy grain. Unknowingly, they meet Joseph, who they fail to recognize, but identifies them. As a test to see if they have truly changed, Joseph requires them to bring back his younger brother, Benjamin, to see if they had hurt him. Also, Joseph keeps one of the brothers, Simeon, as a prisoner until Benjamin is brought to him. Israel resists sending Benjamin since he thinks he is the last of Rachel's offspring. However, the tribe's hunger together with Judah's promise to hold him responsible for bringing Benjamin back home finally forces Israel to let them go.

The brothers present Benjamin to Joseph, collect their grain, free their brother Simeon, and travel back home. Joseph plants a sliver cup in the bag of Benjamin to further test his siblings' attitude. Joseph's steward finds the cup and brings them back to Joseph. The brothers are beside themselves with grief causing Judah to say in Genesis 44:33-34: "'Now then, please let your servant remain here as my lord's slave in place of the boy, and let the boy return with his brothers. How can I go back to my father if the boy is not with me? No! Do not let me see the misery that would come upon my father.'" Judah's compassion and courage convince Joseph that the brothers have changed for the better. Joseph tearfully tells them in Genesis 45:4-5: "'. . . I am your brother Joseph, the one you sold into Egypt! And now, do not be distressed and do not be angry with yourselves for selling me here, because it was to save lives that God sent me ahead of you.'"

We see the change in Joseph from the prideful teenager to a forgiving adult, humbled by ten years of jail and realizing God's plan for him. There is a restoration between the siblings, but not reconciliation as the brothers still don't totally trust Joseph. Such a process will take time as Jeanne Safer points out in her book: "Once siblings are engaged in the reconciliation process, the course is unpredictable for everyone concerned, and nobody has the upper hand or knows in advance where it will lead. There is always a large element of improvisation, miscalculation, and surprise when people repair damaged relationships."

Lesson for us. This story illustrates several factors about the effects of partiality and sibling rivalry:

Parent(s) intentional favoritism can create such envy in the other siblings that they may want to hurt the favored sibling in some way, even in a malicious manner.

The favored one often develops a prideful attitude and sense of entitlement that eventually hurts him and aggravates others.

God is the true healer of favoritism and negative sibling rivalry if the parties involved humbly come to Him, confess their role, and then forgive each other.

Encourage our children to develop and show sibling loyalty with each other instead of sibling rivalry.

The process of restoration from such hatred is not immediate, but requires some time to rebuild a broken trust.

The story of seeking favoritism from Jesus.
Matthew 20:20-28.

Salome, the mother of the apostles, James and John, kneeling before Jesus asked Him for the favor of having her two sons sit on either side of Him in heaven. Since she was Mary's sister, she may have thought that she had a special relationship with Jesus so that her sons deserved such a special privilege. Jesus, realized that such favoritism would be destructive, tells her sons in Matthew 20:22: "'*You don't know what you are asking,' Jesus said to them. 'Can you drink the cup I am about to drink?'*" The two apostles answered yes; unaware of the intense suffering they would later endure: James was martyred and John was exiled for years. Jesus informed them in Matthew 20:23: *"'You will indeed drink from my cup, but to sit on my right or left is not for me to grant. These places belong to those for whom they have been prepared by my father.'"* The mother's action exemplifies many parents' desire to promote their children over others. She is later mentioned as being at the crucifixion, so some commentators believe she remained close to Jesus' family.

Later, the rest of the apostles heard that the mother of James and John tried to advance her sons ahead of them. Quite naturally they became angry with them for this self-advancement plot. Jesus headed off the apostles' anger by enlightening them in Matthew 20:27-28: *"'. . . whoever wants to be great among you must be your servant, and whoever wants to be first must be your slave—just as the Son of Man did not come to be served, but to serve and to give his life as a ransom for many.'"*

Lesson for us. Jesus is telling us not to use family connections, nepotism, to gain positions in God's kingdom. He is asking us to take on the attitude of a humble servant then we can become great in the kingdom of God. This quality is the opposite of the world's standard for greatness of getting all you can get in power and position. Jesus abides by God's admonition to reject any form of favoritism.

Did Jesus show favoritism in selecting Peter, James and John to be in his inner circle?

On the following significant occasions, Jesus selected only these three to be present:

The raising of Jairus's daughter from the dead. As told in Mark 5:35-47, Jairus, a synagogue leader pleaded with Jesus to heal his daughter. On the way there, a messenger reports that the daughter is dead. Jesus proceeds anyway telling them to ignore the message. In verse 5:37: *"He did not let anyone follow him except Peter, James and John the brother of James."* Jesus demonstrated his power over death when He brought the daughter back to life to everyone's astonishment.

The transfiguration of Jesus. As relayed in Matthew 17:1-3, *"After* *six days Jesus took with him Peter, James and John the brother of James, and led them up a high mountain by themselves. There he was transfigured before them. His face shone like the sun and his clothes became a white as the light. Just then there appeared before them Moses and Elijah, talking with Jesus."* Jesus revealed a vision of His radiant glory when we will see Him in heaven as told in Book of Revelation. He showed His true divinity as a part of the Holy Trinity. Charles Spurgeon comments on this: "Another thing which we may learn from our Lord Jesus Christ having shown himself to his apostles, thus robed in brightness is, that we are scarcely aware of the glory of which the human body is capable."

Later in verse 17:5, a cloud envelops them and a voice (the voice of the Father) from the cloud states: *" 'This is my Son, whom I love; with him I am very pleased. Listen to him!'"* Jesus realized that the three disciples didn't fully comprehend what they had seen, which could create confusion, Jesus in verse 17: 9: *"'. . . instructed them 'Don't tell anyone what you have seen until the Son of Man has been raised from the dead.'"* The disciples needed to see Him after the resurrection before they could fully understand. Jesus was just giving His inner circle a preview of the magnificent glory to come.

Praying in the garden of Gethsemane. Jesus in his last night before the crucifixion in Matthew 26:37-38: *"He took Peter and the two sons of Zebedee along with him, and he began to be sorrowful and troubled. Then he said to them, 'My soul is overwhelmed with sorrow to the point of death. Stay here and keep watch with me.'"* Jesus, at his time of greatest stress, realized that he would suffer the anguish of separation from His Father for taking on the sins of all of us plus the horrible physical suffering of his crucifixion. Jesus sought the three for support while He prayed to His Father so intensely that Jesus sweat drops of blood. He knew He needed strength to face His greatest challenge. He returned after prayer to find them sleeping. He asked them again in verse 26:40: *"'. . . Could you men not keep watch with me for one hour?' He asked Peter."* After praying two more times, he returns each time to find them asleep. Imagine the personal pain Jesus may have felt when his three closest earthly friends let him down in His hour of greatest need.

Jesus reveals the deepest personal parts of Himself and nature to just these three: His power over death, His divine glory, and His deep anguish at his coming death. Why just them? Some plausible reasons from Christian commentators are:

Matthew Henry in his "*Commentary on the Bible*" states: "The sons of Zebedee were James and John, two of the first three of Christ's disciples; Peter and they were his favorites; John was the disciple whom Jesus loved; yet none were so often reproved as they; whom Christ loves best he reproves most, Rev.3:19."

Peter, James and John were all fishermen who worked near each other at the Sea of Galilee. James and John were sons of Zebedee (Luke 5:9). The three responded to the call of Jesus at the same time by immediately joining Him. Matt. 4:18-22. All three were strongly motivated to be His followers.

Each of the three was unique in a special way: Peter would be the future head of the Christian church. James became the first Apostle martyred and John would be asked by Jesus to take care of his mother after the crucifixion.

It is natural to have a small group of trustworthy confidants. Jesus sought this small inner circle, rather than all the disciples, to reveal His special attributes and truths. He might have been concerned that these revelations would be too difficult to understand for everyone.

While the three were closest to Jesus, He didn't give them any rewards or favors. The fact is that He tended to rebuke them more than the others, which He would not do if He intentionally favored them.

Some commentators believe Jesus was a cousin of James and John through their mother, Salome, who was the sister of Mary. Consequently, he might have known James and John while growing up and felt comfortable with them.

Summarizing this section, while God the Father and Jesus show a preference for certain people in the Bible, they never demonstrated intentional favoritism with anyone. These preferences probably had to do with each person having a heart for God. David was known as a "man after God's own heart." The Lord speaking in 1 Samuel 16:7

states: "'... *Man looks on the outward appearance, but the Lord looks on the heart.*'" Jesus in the New Testament tells us the greatest command in Matthew 22: 37: "'.... *Love the Lord your God with all your heart and with all your mind and with all your soul...*'" So God knows your heart yet seeks your devotion and responds to those whose hearts yearn for Him.

Lesson for us. Like Jesus, we will prefer some people over others, but like Him we need to avoid employing intentional favoritism. In fact, He was harder on those closest to Him as He expected them to follow through on their spiritual commitment to Him; however their flesh was weak. As Christians, we need to show grace to our fallible humans.

In summary, we see in the Bible that favoritism, especially intentional favoritism, is a sin against God. As a sin we need to treat it seriously and confess it to God seeking His forgiveness and healing. We will all have preferences for certain people over others, but that doesn't mean we don't treat everyone with respect and care. In addition, sibling strife needs to be addressed and sibling loyalty introduced and encouraged. By following these suggestions, we are reflecting Christ to others.

Summary:

1. God condemns favoritism in the Bible. Leviticus 19:15. This theme continues in Exodus 6:7, Proverbs 24:23, Romans 2:11, Colossians 3:25, and James 2:8-9. Examples of partiality in the Old Testament families:

2. **The story of hostile sibling rivalry: Cain and Abel.** Genesis 4:4-6. Both present an offering to God. Abel brings a firstborn, while Cain brings his fruits. Abel's sacrifice is accepted by God but Cain's is rejected. Cain feeling rejected, kills his brother and hides from God.

3. **The story of dual favoritism in the family: Jacob and Esau.** Genesis 25:24-34, 27:1-41, & 28-33:7. This story consists of sibling rivalry plus dual favoritism: Isaac favored Esau and his wife, Rebekah favored Jacob.

a. The two sons were opposites in looks (Esau was physical and hairy while Jacob had smooth skin) and personality (Esau was impetuous while Jacob a quiet conniver). Jacob using a meal conspires to get Isaac's birthright. Later, Jacob with Rebekah's help deceives Isaac into getting his blessing instead of the deserving Esau.

b. Amazingly, 20 years later, they both have become successful and Esau doesn't hold any revenge when they meet again.

4. The story of favoritism and hostile sibling rivalry: Joseph and his brothers.

Genesis 37, 39-45:17. Jacob's (Israel's) blatant favoritism for Joseph is exemplified by giving him a multicolored robe results in the other siblings hating Joseph.

a. Joseph's older siblings plot to kill him, but end up selling him to traveling merchants going to Egypt. Joseph is sold to Pharaoh's captain of the guard, but his wife tries unsuccessfully to lure Joseph into her bedroom. She has Joseph wrongfully jailed. God helps him interpret Pharaoh's two dreams: seven years of prosperity and seven years of drought.

b. Joseph is made second highest in Egypt and put in charge of storing the grain. The drought arrives bringing his brothers to Egypt to buy grain. Joseph recognizes them, but they don't know him.

c. As a test, Joseph requires them to bring back his younger brother, Benjamin, to see if they had hurt him. Joseph tests them by keeping Benjamin to see if they had changed.

d. Judah volunteers to become Joseph's slave instead of Benjamin. Joseph is convinced that the brothers have changed for the better. Joseph reveals himself and welcomes the family to stay. Genesis 45:4-5. This was God's plan to save His people as well as restore Joseph with his brothers.

5. The story of seeking favoritism from Jesus. Salome, the mother of

James and John (Mary's sister) asks Jesus to have them sit with Him in heaven. Because of that familial tie, she thought that her sons deserved special privileges.

a. Jesus, realizing that favoritism is destructive, rejects her request and tells her sons that they will suffer like Him. Matthew 20:22. The other apostles are angry with James and John for the self-advancement attempt. Jesus stops the apostles' anger by telling them that to be great a person must first be a servant. Matthew 20:27-28.

6. Did Jesus show favoritism in selecting Peter, James and John to be his inner circle? On the following occasions, Jesus selected only these three to be present:

a. The raising of Jairus daughter from the dead. Jesus brings the daughter of Jairus, a synagogue leader, back from death. Mark 5:35-47.

b. The transfiguration of Jesus. Jesus reveals a vision of His radiant glory of when He is in heaven. He reveals His true divinity as a part of the Holy Trinity. God acknowledges that Jesus is His son. Matthew 17:1-9.

c. Praying in the garden of Gethsemane. Jesus, the night before His crucifixion, took the three apostles with Him to pray for strength to meet His greatest challenge. He asked them to pray while He prayed so intensely that He sweat drops of blood. They fell asleep every time. Matthew 26:37-38.

d. Some plausible reasons from Christian commentators are:

1). Matthew Henry states: ". . . James and John . . . and Peter . . . were his favorites . . . yet none were so often reproved as they; whom Christ loves best he reproves most, Rev.3:19."

2). Peter, James and John were all fishermen who responded to the call of Jesus at the same time. Matt. 4:18-22.

4). Each was unique: Peter became the future head of the church,

James became the first Apostle martyred and John took care of Mary after the crucifixion.

5). Some commentators believe Jesus was a cousin of James and John through their mother, Salome.

6). Jesus rebuked them more than, which is the opposite of intentional favoritism.

Discussion Questions

1. What reason would you give for God to condemn favoritism?

   How does favoritism relate to God loving people?

2. Do you see any similarity between the people in these Bible stories and favoritism in your life?

3. Do you feel Joseph had the right to test his brothers twice?

   What did you do when you were wronged by your sibling?

   How were you able to reconcile with them?

   What happened to your relationship with them afterward?

4. Do you think that Jesus showed favoritism to Peter, James and John?

   Explain your reasons.

5. What new fact about favoritism did you learn from this chapter?

Chapter 9
Favoritism in the Church

While we were talking about favoritism in the church, Pastor Jonathon told me that his wife had scolded him, "You are favoring Emma in the church by having her pray every time. You can't keep doing that or others will resent it!" He exclaimed, "But she prays so well and with a stirring voice." Jonathon went on to describe how he didn't realize that he was favoring anyone, "It just seemed so easy to just have her pray since I knew what to expect and she did a good job." Jonathon told me how he had learned an important lesson about how easy it is for a Pastor to get caught in the "favoritism cycle." (The cycle is using those same church members to do most of the important work in the church.) He said "I know from experience that they would do things right."

Jonathon discussed how favoritism creeps into the church so easily as he told me about his favorite trustee, usher and ministry leader. He finds himself drawn to people because of their personality and ability. However, he has learned to open up opportunities to others and give them an opportunity to help out to gain better harmony in the church. In addition, more members feel a part of the church and want to help. Now, he has found other members with good abilities that he can rely on.

This true story, with the name changed, reveals how frequently the same church members are asked to do the ministry work, especially the important work. Since the pastor is ultimately held responsible for the performance of all the ministries, he naturally selects those members that he can rely on, or those he prefers. As a result, he has a strong tendency to continue to select the same members without giving others an opportunity. As this "favoritism cycle" continues, the danger is that it creates a special group who could easily begin to think of themselves as the favorites. To maintain the allegiance of this group, the pastor may be inclined to give them rewards, special training and limit disciplining them for mistakes. Gradually with time, they begin to think of themselves as a group of favorites or a clique. They start to exclude others to maintain control of their privileged position.

A dangerous characteristic in most churches, especially larger churches, is the competition between members for the higher positions in the church. People are so accustomed to the competition of the workplace, that they bring that same striving attitude into the church. In fact, many churches even encourage it, despite the Bible condemning it in Romans 12:3: *"For by the grace given me I say to every one of you: Do not think of yourself more highly than you ought, but rather think of yourself with sober judgment, in accordance with the measure of faith God has given you."* The basis of competition is striving to be better than the other person.

It is incompatible to: *"submit to one another out of reverence for Christ,"* as Ephesians 5:21 instructs, while simultaneously trying to better another member in competition for a church position. The "survival of the fittest" concept is not from Scripture, but from the world. The churches that promote or even allow competition to exist often end up with many of the most self-promoting, selfish, and competitive members. The winners of the competition think of themselves as a special group set apart from the majority of the members. These characteristics are the polar opposites of the Christian call to be humble, compassionate, and loving to each other as ourselves. Christianity is not a game to be won, but a challenge to win souls to Christ and disciple them to walk their lives in the fundamental truths of the Bible. Competition needs to be reduced significantly or removed completely from the church for its members to thrive.

Too often those selected for church leadership are determined hastily based on the following:

Selected because they are wealthy. They can help the church financially with large donations. With many churches struggling to stay afloat financially, these wealthy members become very attractive candidates to be selected to important positions. Consequently, they often wield significant power with the pastor and the other leaders in the church. Depending upon their true spiritual state, they can easily lead the church into wrong directions based on human wisdom.

The Bible alerts us to the danger of such a selection in James in 2:1-4: *"Suppose a man comes into your meeting wearing a gold ring and fine clothes, and a poor man in shabby clothes also comes in. If you show special attention to the man wearing the fine clothes and say 'Here's a good seat for you,' but say to the poor man, 'You stand there' or 'Sit on the floor by my feet,' have you not discriminated among yourselves and become judges with evil thoughts?"* Later in James 2:8-9: *"If you really keep the royal law found in Scripture, 'Love your neighbor as yourself,' you are doing right. But if you show favoritism, you sin and are convicted by the law as lawbreakers,"* Thus, favoring a wealthy person is considered a sin. A rich person may be selected for leadership for valid reasons, such a having a true heart for God that is demonstrated in his daily actions over time.

Select those who are professionals or in high worldly positions. We get drawn by people who have become significant in the world. Some examples might be doctors, lawyers, professors etc. While they may have helpful worldly wisdom, such wisdom needs to be subordinated to God's wisdom. This wisdom is what the church needs most in its ministries and leadership.

Select those who appear more "spiritual" than others. The spiritual level of people is difficult to determine. Does it mean those that read the Bible more, pray more sincerely, or speak in tongues? The Bible does not give us clear criteria for spiritual maturity. God is the only one who truly knows a person's spiritual condition.

There are those members who will appear more spiritual through outward performances like: public prayers, prophesying, or speaking in tongues. That does not necessarily make them spiritually mature and/or able to lead a ministry or group. Actions, often those unspoken, done over time will reflect the true attitude and heart.

Those having personalities and interests similar to the pastor. Members that have these characteristic(s) will naturally be attractive to the pastor as friends. The pastor gets to know them and learns to trust them. Also, they are usually supportive of the pastor and his ideas and plans. Consequently, it can be very natural to appoint these friends as ministry leaders even if they may lack important qualifications and spiritual maturity. The downside of this situation is that the pastor gets a group of "yes" leaders who never raise any questions to about what the pastor wants. They too can think of themselves as beyond any discipline and may push limits.

Yet, the Apostle Paul admonishes church leaders when writing to his protégée, Timothy, to guard against favoritism in 1 Timothy 5:21: *"I charge you, in the sight of God and Jesus Christ and the elect angels, to keep these instructions without partiality, and do nothing out of favoritism."* Thus any favoritism by church leaders is against God's word.

We are to neither favor those listed above nor disfavor them, but measure them by godly standards. If any of the above methods is used to select ministry leadership, it can create a group of "special members" that are dysfunctional with favoritism and lack inherent integrity. Soon those outside the special group find that despite how hard and competently they work, they remain excluded. They don't get called to be part of ministry leadership and gain only limited promotions. Consequently, their morale starts to sink, they resent their position, and they reduce their effort. As a last resort, they just leave the church. This sad situation is played out in church after church as their true abilities are never really utilized. In the end, it is both a loss for the church and for the individual. The church's work suffers requiring a few to work harder.

After moving, my wife and I joined a new closer church. At a men's gathering when I first got there, I was warmly welcomed into the group by several men. They discovered that I was a new Christian so they graciously guided me on what to read in the Bible and prayers for my wife and family. With this personal attention, I became very motivated to help in several ministries: Men's Ministry, ushering, and Sunday school.

I strived to learn what was required and to perform at my best as I felt that God was with me in my efforts. My wife also came in with the same enthusiasm and worked in the Sunday school with children. One day, my wife joyfully exclaimed to me in relief, "At last we've found our church home after trying all those other churches."

The Men's Ministry was led by a man who ran it by himself and was one of the elders in the church. He had some good ideas, which included getting the men together for occasional breakfasts and a men's retreat. However, within three years he was struggling to keep up with the demands of the ministry. Our meetings began to be delayed and in his last year, the men's retreat was cancelled. He did all the work himself and did not train any other men to help him. The stress wore him out, so he quit.

The Pastor wisely decided to select three men, who were elders, to head up the ministry as a team. Working together they developed new ideas and were able to divide the workload among themselves. Soon we had monthly breakfasts that grew steadily in number. Then another man and myself joined the team. I felt so excited by this new challenge and told my wife, "I think I've found my calling to minister to men. I feel so exhilarated by this opportunity!" Additionally, I felt more a part of the church by having this particular responsibility. I attended every planning meeting that was held. It was a joy to see all five of us working together as a team. Soon, I was actively making suggestions to enhance the ministry.

Within two years, two of the leaders had moved, but the ministry never missed a step as our breakfasts grew to over 30 men with men attending from other churches. As a result, the men of the church enjoyed a true excitement from the meaningful meetings that we had.

Proposed is a different selection process that gives more members opportunities for ministry positions:

1. Does the person have a servant's heart? Jesus stated such a principle in Matthew 20:26-28: "'. . . *whoever wants to be first must be your slave—just as The Son of Man did not come to be served, but to serve, and to give his life as a ransom for many.*'" The principle of being a servant first is so important as it teaches humility and obedience. Such lessons drive out the human tendency for pride and striving for position. Once the servant attitude is a part of a person's character, they are equipped by God for higher service.

2. Review their performance and attitude over time. Start them working in a ministry as trainees. Over time you can see their true attitudes and abilities to conduct themselves in a godly way. Measure their performance using objective measurements not skewed by human opinions. This opportunity allows them to gain valuable experience in a church ministry. It permits them to see how ministry management is done, both positively and negatively. Then they are ready for promotion.

3. Use management teams instead of single mangers for ministry leadership. My story above outlines many of the advantages of such a system. When a single person is put in charge of a ministry, the chance for failure significantly multiplies. Also, what is the path for continuity when that person leaves for some reason? The pressure to perform on only one person can be overwhelming; while capable others are allowed to let their skills languish. Churches usually get caught up in this authoritarian style of leadership that even most businesses have discarded as unworkable, as the team approach is far more effective.

In fact, Jesus used teams to accomplish ministry work as in Luke 10:1-2: *"After this the Lord appointed seventy-two others and sent them two by two ahead of him to every town and place where he was about to go. The harvest is plentiful, but the workers are few . . ."* Later in Luke 10:17 they successfully returned: *"The seventy-two returned with joy and said, 'Even the demons submit in your name.'"* He used the twelve apostles and other followers, but never set one above the others.

One of the most destructive ways favoritism becomes entrenched in the church is allowing cliques to take over different ministries. A clique is defined by *Webster's* as, "a narrow exclusive circle or group of persons." Their exclusiveness comes about by the leaders not allowing outsiders into leadership or setting directions for the group. Their leadership's tight control prohibits listening to the ideas or opinions of those outside their circle. Outsiders are allowed to help the ministry by doing only the grunt and/or unseen work with limited or no affirmation or reward. They have little or no hope of promotion.

Additionally, the clique leadership feels immune to any discipline or correction. The result is those on the outside feel: excluded, unfavored, angry, and under utilized. Such a situation creates divisiveness in the church that breeds a rippling discontent. It also is against the royal law that James 2:8, quoted above, states: *". . . love your neighbor as yourself."* Consequently, cliques are against God's desire and commandment.

Josh and Edith joined the church with a new hope of finding a friendly church. Initially, everyone they encountered was welcoming and encouraging. They entered into different ministries with Josh going into the program for boys along with their eight-year-old son. Edith joined the young girl's program along with their six-year-old daughter. They both assisted in those programs where they had previous experience. Each noticed how their respective ministry seemed to be led by a small controlling group.

After six months of helping, Josh started making what he thought were some helpful suggestions. They were all rebuffed as he was told: "We really don't want your ideas. We know what we are doing as we've being doing it this way for 15 years." Afterward, the ministry leader started shunning him by not interacting with him. Apparently, this was a typical tactic that he had used before on others to quiet them and maintain his rigid control.

Shocked at this put down, later Josh felt the strong atmosphere of constraint when helping in the ministry. He asked God: "Why is this happening to me? I'm only trying to do my best as I love working with the young boys. I just want to help!" Edith also felt the same thing happening in her ministry, as the church seemed to be controlled by several cliques. No one seemed to stand up to them. So after a year of being shunned, Josh had had enough and sadly his family left the church.

In such a church, such painful examples will be multiplied until the leadership finally grasps the problem and tries to address it. If not corrected quickly, the church will usually undergo massive defections, which finally forces the leadership to take action. In fact, behavior like this can cause the church to fall apart completely, which has happened in some cases. Some suggestions of ways to remove favoritism from the church and keep it in check involve the following:

1. The pastor speaks to the congregation on the definition and dangers of intentional favoritism. He declares that he will not

allow intentional favoritism to exist in the church; he will find it and stop it.

2. He asks the elders to inform him immediately of any evidence now, or in the future of intentional favoritism. He encourages the parishioners to bring any evidence of favoritism to an elder, who will have it thoroughly investigated. Once it has been established that intentional favoritism has taken place, the pastor will take action.

3. Show the established leaders what they are losing by using intentional favoritism and its negative effects on members of their group. If the ministry leaders still refuse to change their approach, it will become necessary to insert new leadership to break up entrenched cliques. Have the performance of all members measured objectively without subjective input. Establish a pattern of promotion and training for all newer members. Require term limits for leaders. Tell the new leaders they should seriously consider the ideas of new group members. Continue to monitor the group's situation for positive changes.

4. Insure that rewards, training and affirmation are spread around to many different members and not always to a select few.

5. Don't be afraid to discipline any member if they are found to have demonstrated favoritism on a regular basis. As Colossians 3:25 says: "*Anyone who does wrong will be repaid for his wrong, and there is no favoritism.*" For example you could have them study the Bible and write about what it says about favoritism, how they could avoid using favoritism in the future, be more humble, impartial, and displaying a servant's attitude.

Steps a church member can take where intentional favoritism is reigning in a church or ministry are:

Pray for the church or ministry. Ask God to remove the favoritism from the church and/or ministry. He will direct you on how to act and what to say when you are incurring partiality. Often we get so frustrated with it that we become angry and comment harshly about it to someone. Remember that God hates favoritism and eventually will take action against the offenders.

Be patient yet persevere in your ministry. You often lose hope when partiality continues to affect you without any correction being made. Continue to do your best in the ministry. God may be using this situation to refine your character and build your perseverance. Also, He acts in His time frame, not ours. You will tend to get impatient particularly when wrongdoing has been happening for a while. Read Psalms (i.e. 18, 27, and 31) that give you hope while going through a trial. If there is still no change, go to the next step.

Speak to an understanding elder. Speak to an elder with whom you are comfortable and is a sympathetic listener. Help him/her to see not only your situation, but how that intentional favoritism is against the Word of God and can endanger the church. Explain how many are being negatively affected by this partiality. Remember elders may be reluctant to face the issue. If there is no change proceed to the next step.

Speak to the pastor. Tell him of the situation, how you have been unfavored with specific examples, and what steps you have taken. Formulate your ideas as questions as they are less confrontational. Explain how the Bible condemns favoritism and ask for his advice. Does he really listen and understand you or does he try to make excuses for the favoritism of the ministry leadership? Too often the pastor becomes defensive about ministry leaders as he may have promoted them. Does he deny or face the situation? Real healing only comes from facing issues and dealing with them in a godly way. If there is still no change, you have the following options:

Continue to stay and pray for a change. You will, however, need to find an outlet for your anger by talking with a trusted close friend. Your anger could eat you up and/or cause you to say or do something destructive to someone. Continue to pray for change, but remember that change often takes a long time in many of these situations. There is a general inertia against change in most churches. If you are willing to put up with the abuse, change will eventually come.

Most people find another church. They feel relieved to be away from that destructive situation. They may go to another church or not go at all feeling disillusioned by the painful experience. It is so sad that the latter occurs too often. Ironically, sometimes they return to their original church after the leadership changes have been made and the favoritism has been removed.

Summary:

1. A Pastor, because of his responsibility for the performance of the church ministries, has a strong tendency to select the same members which creates a "favoritism cycle." This group thinks of themselves as favorites.

2. The pastor gives them rewards, special training but limits disciplining them. The group becomes a clique that excludes others and maintains control of their position.

3. Usual criteria for selecting for church leadership are the following:

a. The wealthy. They can financially help the church. Depending upon their spiritual state, they can lead in wrong directions based on human wisdom. James 2:1-4 and James 2:1-4 tell us that favoring the wealthy is a sin. They may be selected for leadership, but should demonstrate a true heart for God.

b. The professionals or those in high worldly positions. Examples are: doctors, lawyers, professors etc. They have helpful worldly wisdom that needs to be subordinated to God's wisdom.

c. Those who are more "spiritual." The spiritual level of people is difficult to determine. The Bible lacks specific criteria on it; God only knows a person's heart. Unspoken actions over time reflect the true attitude and heart.

d. Those having personalities and interests similar to the Pastor. These characteristics often become friends with the Pastor, who trusts them. They get appointed as ministry leaders despite lacking qualifications. The downsides are they always agree with the pastor and think they are beyond discipline.

4. This above means of selecting ministry leaders creates a group of "special members." Outsiders eventually discover, however, that despite how hard they work, they remain excluded. They may get limited promotions, but they are never allowed to lead a ministry. Their morale sinks and they reduce their effort. Finally, they leave the church. It is a loss for both the church and the families.

5. Suggestions for a proposed different selection process for ministry leadership:

a. Above all the person must have a servant's heart. Jesus, in Matthew 20:26-28, states the principle of first being a servant before leading. It teaches that humility helps to reduce human pride.

b. Review their performance and attitude over time. Start them as trainees. Review their attitudes and abilities to conduct themselves using objective measurements. They gain experience how ministry management is done.

c. Use teams for ministry leadership. A single leader of a ministry has a significant chance of failure which hurts continuity. The pressure on one person is overwhelming while capable others languish in neglect. The authoritarian style has been found unworkable. Jesus used teams for ministry work see Luke 10:1-2 and Luke 10:17.

6. Favoritism becomes entrenched in different ministry cliques. They exclude outsiders from the leadership circle and ignore their ideas. Outsiders only get the grunt work with no affirmation. Outsiders feel: excluded, unfavored, angry, and under utilized. It creates a rippling discontent throughout the church and is against God's royal law.

7. Suggestions to remove favoritism from the church and keep it in check are:

1. The pastor speaks to the members on the dangers of favoritism and declares that he will stop it.

2. He asks elders to inform him immediately of any favoritism. He wants the members to bring any favoritism to an elder, who will investigate it. The results are brought to the pastor for action.

3. Break up any entrenched ministry cliques by: inserting new leadership, require promotion, training for new members, and establish term limits for leaders. Have the performance of members is measured only objectively. If the clique leaders refuse to change, remove them and keep monitoring the group.

4. Insure that rewards, training and affirmation are given to many members.

5. Discipline those members that regularly demonstrate favoritism. Require them to: study the Bible about favoritism, write on the dangers of favoritism, avoid favoritism in the future, and become humble.

Steps to consider if you have favoritism in your church or ministry:

Pray for the church or ministry. Ask God to remove the favoritism. Seek His direction when faced with it. God hates favoritism and ask Him to remove it.

Be patient yet persevere in your ministry. Continue to do your best in the ministry. God may be building perseverance in you and acts in His time frame. To gain hope read Psalms (i.e. 18, 27, and 32). If no change, go to the next step.

Speak to an understanding elder. Speak to a kindly deacon who is a good listener. Tell them of the favoritism and how others are being negatively affected. He may not want to face the issue. If no change, go to the next step.

Speak to the pastor. Tell him of specific examples of favoritism, and your previous steps. Formulate your points as questions and ask for his advice. Explain how the Bible condemns favoritism. Does he face the situation? If no change, you have the following options:

> **Continue to stay and pray for a change.** Find a trusted close friend to discuss your anger. Continue to pray for change remembering it may take years because of inertia. If you wait long enough, change will eventually come.

> **Find another church.** Most people feel relieved to be away from the situation. They may go to another church or even not go at all. Sometimes they return after the leadership changes and the favoritism is removed.

Discussion Questions

1. Are you in a church/ministry that has intentional favoritism?

   If so, what do your plan to do something about it?

   Have you tried any of the steps outlined above?

   What were the results?

2. Are you unfavored or overlooked in church?

   What can you do about changing the situation?

3. If you are involved in church leadership, what can you do to remove favoritism?

   Are the above steps for selecting leadership helpful?

4. Quote two verses that apply to partiality in the church.

   Explain what they mean to you.

Chapter 10
Favoritism in the Workplace

"And masters, treat your slaves (employees) *in the same way. Do not threaten them, since you know that he who is both their Master and yours is in heaven, and there is no favoritism with him."* (Ephesians 6:9). Note (employees) added by the author for clarification.

A major segment of our waking hours is spent working at our jobs where many of our real struggles with favoritism arise. Of the many people that I have interviewed for this book, all of them remembered favoritism in the workplace leaving lasting, painful memories. A study conducted by Georgetown University McDonough School of Business reported in August 2011 that 92% of 303 senior corporation executives surveyed had witnessed favoritism in promotions at their companies. Paradoxically, the same study stated that 72% of the respondents say that their companies require objective evaluations. Lamentably, favoritism seems to reign in the workplace. When this condition occurs to adults, they remember the painful details quickly and for a longer time (see Chapter 7 covering adult partiality).

I had been working hard at the bank in New York City for 10 years and had slowly been promoted. I had been asked to head up the bank's Upstate New York Real Estate Region. Initially, I had no employees and no customers. Our bank had just opened offices for the first time across Upstate. I was told by my boss: "You have three years to make the office profitable or you are out of a job." Consequently, I hit the road to get customers and within three months I was blessed to get my first one in Rochester. Later that year, I was truly blessed to get a major shopping center loan that made us profitable enabling me to feel relieved for my job.

Frequently, I had to travel back to headquarters in NYC for loan approvals and discussions about marketing strategy. I was deeply hoping to get my final promotion to Vice President. Such a promotion was a major career step, but it was also important in being welcomed by most major customers. In addition, I felt that I had earned it with our office becoming profitable so quickly. My boss, who I very much admired at the time, told me: "Don't worry about it, I promise you that you will get it this year. Just don't bug me about it again!" So I didn't mention the promotion to him again. I just patiently waited for my review date when the promotion was usually given. At the same time, I noticed that my boss was having frequent long discussions with a younger counterpart who came into the department four years after I did.

When the promotion date came, I didn't get the promotion, but my younger counterpart did. I couldn't believe that I didn't get the promotion, but that he gave it to my younger counterpart. I felt deeply deceived by my boss's failure to honor his promise to me about the promotion and furious for being misled by him. My boss's response was, "I don't remember promising you that promotion" then, he curtly dismissed me. I then realized that my boss and this younger counterpart were the only Jewish bankers in the Department. As I saw them going off together to celebrate, I realized in the business world that: "it is not what you know or accomplish, but who you know." Fortunately, I was given a new boss who recognized my achievements by promoting me the next year.

I am sure many of you have also faced the anguish of partiality in the workplace. It leaves painful scars in its victims that can affect them for the rest their lives and damages the business as well. Some favoritism will always exist because of our human frailty to prefer some people over others. The sources of dysfunctional favoritism in the workplace are similar to those found in the church, but slightly different:

Nepotism. It comes from the Italian word meaning nephew. It means favoring family members for promotions and raises. We see this happening particularly in family businesses, or where one family has a large interest in the company. I can remember a fellow worker who had married into the Rockefeller family was constantly favored at my bank.

Cronyism. It refers to a partiality toward personal associates and friends. This situation is more frequent and creates a climate where subordinates vie for a relationship with the boss. The winners become part of the "insider's group" with whom the authority begins to spend a lot of time.

Similar personality. Such a characteristic naturally draws people together as they have the same feelings and thoughts. There is a special kinship that develops between the boss and subordinate. This attribute can easily lead to cronyism. An authority just feels comfortable with this type of subordinate.

Similar interests. The employee having similar interests as the boss such as: golf, fishing, hunting (usually for male bosses), crafts, and Facebook (usually for female bosses). They bring the subordinate and boss together in a friendly environment where the boss can appreciate the employee in a different way. These interests create a new connection with the boss outside of work.

Similar values. These values can be faith based like both being Christian, Moslem, or Jewish etc. On the other hand they or can be based on evil values like drugs or sexual escapades. Our values are such an important part of our lives that they draw us close to those of like values. I can remember a boss who's Christian faith drew me to him as I felt so comfortable working under him.

When I joined the Real Estate Division, the leader was a devoted Christian with a large family. Immediately, I felt a kinship with him because of his faith and values. I was excited by our various discussions on family values. While demanding of each of us, he encouraged us to learn and grow.

Later, he selected me over several other employees to set up and manage the first regional office of the Real Estate Department. I felt so honored that he had selected me. He told me, "I knew I could trust you to do a good job and be successful." I did my best not to let him down and later proved to be a success.

Education or position. Some businesses hire graduates from specific universities, like the Ivy League schools. They feel that they are smarter and may have more wealthy contacts for the business. As a result, they are often "fast tracked" for promotion and their careers. Like many favorites, they soon feel entitled and start to coast on their favored position. Later, they may wonder why they were fired.

Gender, race and ethnicity. "Support your own," is a phase that some minority bosses use to favor their members over other more capable candidates. Like my story above, minority bosses feel justified in their actions because of past injustices in hiring, rightful promotions, and rewards. As reimbursement, they overcompensate their fellow minority member with greater rewards than others.

All of the above means of selecting favorites may seem justified by the boss at the time. It may be happening so subtly that the boss is not even aware of it. It is when favoritism becomes blatant or intentional that it truly becomes destructive to the favorite, the boss, the unfavored employees, and the company. Blatant favoritism arises when an employee is given: greater bonuses, more affirmation, faster raises and promotions than equally qualified employees because they are liked by the boss. Also, they are not disciplined when they do wrong. It is when a combination of these actions occurs over time that blatant favoritism is confirmed. Otherwise it could just be the competent hard work of an employee. The consequences of blatant (toxic) favoritism on a business are as follows:

A loss of morale by the unfavored. Since there are many more employees that are a part of the "outside group," this loss of morale usually reduces overall production and effort. They recognize that hard work and competence is not recognized. It can easily thwart the goals of the business and result in its profits falling. Morale, the same as one's attitude, is a critical component to an employee's quality of work, his satisfaction, and effort.

A loss of capable employees. Frustrated employees will just leave the business if they feel they are not appreciated with promotions, raises, training, and praise. In fact, affirmation is often the most important reward to an employee, while most bosses think raises are the most important. A combination of both is the best, when possible.

The favorite doesn't try his best. Because of his/her favored position, the favorite will try to get away with less effort on the job. As a result, the quality of his/her work may diminish as he/she "cuts corners." The boss may permit this situation to continue for a while, but bosses get changed and it will be discovered. Such a meager effort can easily become a habit by the favorite thereby sowing the seeds of his/her destruction.

The favorite believes they can avoid all correction. The favorite's belief arises from the boss's reluctance to discipline him/her at all. They realize their privileged position causes them to push past the company's boundaries. Once discipline comes, they are usually shocked at the results.

Discrimination of minorities. When someone belongs to a minority, they often encounter discrimination in hiring, promotions, raises and praise. The authority who discriminates against an employee fails to recognize that real talent and abilities has no skin color, gender or ethnic background. The pain of this type of prejudice leaves a lasting anger and frustration in the worker. It denies the business of the benefits of some of its best talent. James 2:4: *"Have you not discriminated among yourselves and become judges with evil thoughts?"*

These actions are illegal, but are often difficult to prove. Today's culture and most corporate Human Research Departments are very sensitive to such actions and they move to quickly remove them. However, they continue particularly in small businesses as reflected in the story below:

Mona, an African-American woman in her thirties, had received a certificate of completion from a major culinary school and had worked for restaurants for five years. She had strong practical and educational background for her next promotion at the restaurant. However, a less experienced white man without the same education got the job. She was so angry, but she talked with the owner who claimed: "You just need more experience. You're doing a good job just keep it up." She was convinced that her race and gender were the real difference.

In frustration she left shortly thereafter and discovered the same situation occurring. She asked God: "Why does this keep happening to me?" Finally, she got depressed and started using drugs. She came to Teen Challenge for the help that she needed. She started to depend upon God on a more regular basis and felt His direction renewed her confidence. Afterward, she found a restaurant owner who finally appreciated her culinary skills and made her the head cook.

In the workplace, each of us has been or is in one of the following categories: favored, unfavored, and overlooked employees. Our position as overlooked or unfavored probably resulted in personal agony in our lives. Below are some helpful suggestions for you to minimize the effect of partiality in your workplace:

Being the favorite. You can take several different steps to reduce favoritism in your workplace as follows:

> **Ask God how you can change the situation.** This point is first because He knows the true condition of you in your workplace. When favoritism is reigning, Satan is working effectively to ruin lives. God wants to change the environment and reduce or remove the partiality, but He may not do it immediately. That doesn't mean that He won't act, but He will in His own timing.

> **Share your workload.** Ask your boss to let you share some of your important work, not grunt work, with another employee who is overlooked or even unfavored. A helpful concept is to bring them into your team, which will give them another opportunity to demonstrate their true abilities to the boss. Hopefully the boss may see them in a more positive way and change his negative opinion of them.

> **Share the praise with others.** When you are affirmed, spread the praise to the others that helped you, particularly those who are unfavored or overlooked. This action will bolster their self-esteem and set an example for other favored employees to do the same. You will feel an inner joy from the Lord for your kindness.

> **Be honest and trustworthy.** As a favorite you may have used lies and deceit to get ahead, which too often is the way of the world. Commit to not following that path as it will lead you to ruin. "Let your word be your bond" regardless of the circumstances as you will

then be walking with God in the truth and not the lies of Satan.

Emphasize the team approach. Working within a team diminishes your favoritism, since the whole team works together to accomplish the goals. The contributions from each member are critically important for the team's success. Likewise the letdown of one member can cause the team's defeat. To overcome this, team members often step in and work with the faltering member to improve their performance to help the team to reach its goals.

Speak to your boss or Human Resources. Being a favorite has its destructive downside as follows: selfishness, greed for more rewards, loss of relationships with cohorts, a desire to break rules, pride, and the loss of relationship with God. Therefore, you will want to change your position. Ask Human Resources on how you can correct your situation of being a favorite.

Don't accept all the rewards given. Instead recommend giving them to other deserving cohorts who may have helped you become successful. They will greatly appreciate such a gesture and it will improve your teamwork. Giving to others always helps to remove greed and a desire for more rewards. Proverbs 11:24: *"One man gives freely, yet gains even more; another withholds unduly, but comes to poverty."*

Being an unfavored or overlooked employee. Some suggestions to improve your situation:

Seek spiritual strength. God cares for you and your pain when you are in this position. He wants to help you if you reach out to Him through sincere prayer and through His Word. There are some 40 Psalms that speak to overcoming trials, like: Psalms 69, 71, and 86. Psalm 34:18 states: *"The LORD is close to the brokenhearted and saves those who are crushed in spirit."*

Determine if you are really a victim. The employee who seems favored may have just outperformed you. Try to get the objective truth from a trusted friend, or two. Try objectively as possible to compare your performance with that of the favorite.

Ask the boss for new opportunities or training. This approach is taking the positive step to improve your performance. At the same time, you show the boss that you don't harbor "sour grapes" over the apparent partiality. Ask the boss on some practical ways that you could improve your performance. Such an action reflects a positive attitude and your desire to get better, which most bosses appreciate.

Do not address the favoritism issue with the boss as it usually backfires. Also, don't gossip at work about it. Divulge your hurt feelings to a close friend or spouse. You don't want the boss to hear about your pain.

Don't reveal your anger at the favorite. You should remain friendly, but somewhat distant. If the favored employee is your friend, your friendship will struggle. In any case, try not to reveal your inner emotions to officemates on this issue.

Don't let it negatively affect your performance. This step is hard to do since you feel your real performance was not judged fairly. By reducing your performance, you only confirm to the boss that he made the right choice. Ask God to help you to at least maintain a positive job performance despite your painful disappointment.

Accept correction willingly. As employees, sometimes we inadvertently do or fail to do things that irritate the boss. Consequently, we become unfavored at least temporarily. It is so important to accept the correction and take the positive steps needed to turn a negative situation into a positive for your career. Below is my story.

I had been transferred from NYC to Syracuse, NY to run a Region of the Real Estate Dept. On one of my frequent trips to the main office, my boss called me into his office. He proceeded to read off a list of minor things that he felt I was doing wrong. Caught off guard, my initial reaction was to be defensive, but I caught myself before I said anything.

Instead, I remembered what my father told me to accept the correction as the boss is expecting a defensive response. I asked the boss: "If you were given the same list of corrections, how would you handle them?" Amazingly, he proceeded to tell me every corrective step to take. I thanked him and immediately proceeded to follow his advice. Within two months, my boss couldn't say enough good things about me and later I got a sizeable raise.

Try to maintain a positive attitude. A negative attitude is usually sensed by a boss and is very destructive to you. You may have lost hope for your future in that workplace and feel depressed. The answer is to seek encouragement from the following sources: prayer to God, reading Bible verses on encouragement, talking with an understanding spouse, and also a dear listening friend. These are your true sources of strength in times of trial.

Be patient. The success of favorites will sometimes prove to be an illusion as their performance deteriorates over time. They may have been promoted beyond their capabilities or mistakenly feel they don't have to keep producing results. Thus, you need to be ready and performing at your best for the boss to consider you as his replacement. As mentioned earlier, there are many downsides to favoritism for the favorite. Colossians 1:10-11: *"And we pray this in order that you may live a life worthy of the Lord and please him in every way . . . being strengthened with all power according to his glorious might so that you may have great endurance and patience . . ."*

As a last resort, talk to Human Resources. You are trying not to be a tattletale, but seek information on how to handle the situation from someone with experience. Since favoritism is so widespread, HR has had plenty of experience dealing with it effectively. See if they would introduce more objective measurements of your performance and limit the subjective evaluation segments. They may have had similar complaints about the same boss, so they will want to correct the situation because of the many negative effects on the company.

The spiritual step is the most important and should be attempted first. Try some of the remaining steps and see if your present condition improves. If there still is no change, try the last steps. By trying them in a piecemeal manner, you will be more effective and not feel overloaded.

Summary:

1. The sources of favoritism in the workplace are:

a. Nepotism. It means favoring family members for promotions and raises.

b. Cronyism. Partiality toward personal associates and friends where subordinates vie for a relationship with the boss.

c. Similar personality. The boss and the employee develop a special kinship.

d. Similar interests. The employee has similar interests that bring the subordinate and boss together.

e. Similar values. These values can be faith based, just valuing hard work, or evil values like drugs or sexual escapades.

f. Education or position. Some businesses seek new hires from Ivy League schools are "fast tracked" for careers, but often fail because of their favored position.

g. Gender, race and ethnicity. Some minority bosses favor minority employees over other capable candidates. They over compensate for their fellow minority members.

2. Blatant favoritism is when an employee is given: greater rewards and more praise than other qualified employees because the boss likes them. They receive no discipline.

Blatant favoritism results in:

a. A loss of morale by the unfavored. Their low morale reduces production and can cause profits to drop. Hard work is not recognized.

b. A loss of capable employees. Frustrated employees leave as they are not appreciated.

c. The favorite doesn't try his best. The favorite tries giving less effort with lower quality. Eventually this situation is discovered and they are fired.

d. The favorite believes they can avoid all correction. The boss doesn't discipline the favorite so he/she breaks company's boundaries.

e. Discrimination of minorities. Minorities encounter discrimination in hiring and rewards creating long-term anger and denies the business of excellent talent. These actions are illegal. James 2:4.

3. Being the favorite. Several steps to reduce favoritism:

1). Ask God how you can change your situation. God knows the true condition in your workplace. He will remove the partiality in His time.

2). Share your workload. Share some of your important work with another overlooked or unfavored employee. Bring them into your team allowing them to demonstrate their true abilities. This action may change the boss's negative impression of that employee.

3). Share the praise with others. Spread any praise you receive to others who helped you—particularly the unfavored or overlooked ones. It will bolster their self-esteem and give them an inner joy.

4). Be honest and trustworthy. Commit to telling the truth. Let God guide you to walking in the truth and not in the lies of Satan.

5). Emphasize the team approach. Working within a team diminishes your favoritism. Each member's contributions are critical for the team's success.

6). Speak to your boss or Human Resources. Being the favorite has its downside: selfishness, greed, loss of relationships with cohorts and God, breaking rules, and pride. Ask HR on how you can change this situation.

7). Don't accept all the rewards given. Instead recommend other deserving cohorts who have helped you. They will appreciate your gesture. Proverbs 11:24.

4. Being an unfavored or overlooked employee. Some suggestions to improve your situation:

1). Seek spiritual strength. God cares for your pain so try to reach out to Him through: prayer and Bible reading. Psalms 69, 71, 86, and 34:18.

2). Determine if you are really a victim. The employee who seems favored may have outperformed you. Find the truth from a friend.

3). Ask the boss for new opportunities or training. Ask the boss about positive steps to improve your performance. Don't tell the boss that you are bitter over his partiality, as it usually backfires. Tell your hurt feelings to a close friend or spouse.

4). Don't reveal your anger at the favorite. You should remain friendly, but somewhat distant. Try not to reveal your inner emotions to officemates.

5). Don't let it negatively affect your performance. This step is hard to do. Reducing your performance only confirms the boss's choice. Ask God to help you to maintain your performance.

6). Accept correction willingly. It is important to accept the correction and take the positive steps to turn a negative situation into a positive.

7). Try to maintain a positive attitude. A negative attitude is discerned by the boss and is destructive to you. Seek encouragement from: God, Bible verses on encouragement, a spouse, and a listening friend.

8). Be patient. The favorite's success may be temporary as he /she may have been promoted beyond their capabilities or they stop producing. You need to perform at your best for the boss to consider you as his/her replacement.

9). As a last resort, talk to Human Resources. Seek information on how to deal with favoritism from HR. Ask if they would introduce objective measurements of your performance. They may have had similar complaints about the same boss.

Start with the spiritual step first, then try the remaining steps and see if your condition improves. Then try the remaining steps.

Discussion Questions

1. Have you or are you encountering favoritism in your workplace?

   If so, what type?

   What do your feel about it?

2. If so, what spiritual steps have you taken to help you?

   Have they improved the situation?

3. Are you the unfavored or overlooked one in your workplace?

   What have you done to change that?

4. Have you used any of the steps suggested above?

   What were they?

   What were the results?

5. Did you talk with HR about the partiality? What suggestions did they give you?

    When you tried them did, they help you improve your perspective and/or situation?

6. If you were made the boss, what actions would you take to remove favoritism?

Chapter 11
How to Reduce Favoritism in Our Lives

Favoritism is a fact in each of our lives that occurs in every family, or group. The prospect of becoming a favorite is so enticing to each of us because it impersonates a form of love. It is when favoritism becomes intentional that it becomes destructive to the favorite, the unfavored one, and the overlooked one. Intentional favoritism develops when the authority in a group uses superficial ways to get a child or member to strive for the authority's goals that are for his/her benefit. This selfish action often does not benefit the favorite over the long term. As we have seen from the previous chapters, intentional favoritism, if allowed to exist has and will affect our lives in many destructive ways. To review, here are some examples:

Impairs, or even destroys, our relationship with Jesus. As Christians we treasure our daily relationship with Jesus. He is our main source of strength, joy, and direction. Jesus confirms this when talking to his apostles in John 15:5-6: *"'I am the Vine; you are the branches. If a man remains in me and I in him, he will bear much fruit; apart from me you can do nothing. If anyone does not remain in me, he is like a branch that is thrown away and withers; such branches are picked up, thrown into the fire and burned.'"* We know we need to maintain that close relationship if we are to flourish as Christians in our lives.

Striving to be the favorite, whether in the family, church or workplace, usually distracts us from this life-saving relationship with Jesus. Additionally, seeking partiality can cause us to put worldly goals ahead of Christ and thereby violate the first commandment, Exodus 20:3: *"'You shall have no other gods before me.'"*

Ruptures your relationships with family or friends. Favoritism often divides us from those closest to us: whether it be other members of the family or friends. When we hear the other family member or friend is constantly praised, rewarded, promoted etc. by our mutual authority, it can cause us to feel frustrated and angry. The irony is that we usually blame the favored family member or friend, when in reality the partiality was initiated by the authority. When this happens, you can take some of the positive steps mentioned above, like seeking God's help, to secure strength to endure the circumstances.

Brings a sense of entitlement. In our human hearts, we all want to be liked and affirmed. A characteristic of favoritism is the more attention we receive the more we want. Soon we learn to expect it constantly from the authority person and we begin to treat unfavored and overlooked ones as inferior to ourselves. We become very prideful and believe we are so vital to the family, church or workplace. We start to think: "We don't have to do the menial work; those others should do all of it. I'm above that."

Purposely breaks boundaries. Favorites feel so entitled that they feel that they are above the rules. To prove this point, they will sometimes purposely break them, expecting no correction. If their actions are permitted to continue, they will eventually end up devastating their lives and achievements. By breaking society's rules, they can be stopped through public disgrace or even going to jail, or prison as well, for society's sake. Proverbs 16:18: *"Pride goes before destruction, a haughty spirit before a fall."*

Everyone seeks become a favorite. Since the favorites usually get most of the major awards, promotions and praise, every person has a prevailing incentive to become a "favorite." Every member becomes focused on achieving that goal and defeat others from attaining it. They may use underhanded, evil tactics such as lying, cheating, and putting others down, to win. The environment soon turns into a "survival of the fittest," breaking down the members' cooperation within any team. The individual's goal of achieving the favored status becomes the priority over any team goals. As a result, the group or organizational goals usually are not reached causing everyone to lose and the organization to possibly fail.

People become self-centered. As favorites they expect to get almost anything they desire. Once they start getting their wishes filled with things, their desires expand to want more. However, they only achieve a fleeting satisfaction, before they want something else. Dr. Les Carter in his book, *The Anger Trap,* speaks about this: "It provokes the individual to become so inwardly focused that the ability to tend to the feelings and needs of others is lost."

All these temporal things lack the true satisfaction that deep personal joy and love between God, family, and friends brings to us all. These are the sources of true fulfillment. Solomon spoke of this condition in Ecclesiastes 2:1: "*I thought in my heart, 'Come now, I will test you with pleasure to find out what is good.' But that also proved to be meaningless.*" Later, Solomon reveals the true answer to life in Ecclesiastes 12:13: "*Now all has been heard; here is the conclusion of the matter: Fear God and keep his commandments, for this is the whole duty of man.*"

The time proven principles below, if followed over time, will help alleviate these negative consequences of intentional favoritism listed above. To become effective several of these principles will need to be followed by the individual and/or the group leader. They are:

Using cooperation versus competition in groups. Our society and culture believe strongly in the intrinsic value of competition in selecting those best performing players or workers, who often become the favorites. Competition starts in the home with parents having their children vie for attention and praise. It continues into school and later in the workplace. Sadly, it thrives in churches, especially large churches, with many members seeking positions of power. Competition creates a few winners, but many more losers who quickly become resentful of their condition. Their ideas aren't considered and their work is not truly appreciated. As a result, they become apathetic in their attendance, work effort, and quality of work. Often they end up leaving the group or company out of silent protest.

Cooperation is when all parties work together to achieve a common goal. Everyone's ideas are welcomed and considered so that they feel a part of the success of the group. Paul in 1 Corinthians 12:14 highlights cooperation: *"For the body is not made up of one part, but many. If the foot should say, 'Because I am not a hand, I do not belong to the body,' it would not for that reason cease to be part of the body."* And later summarized in verse 20: *"As it is, there are many parts, but one body."* Thus, everyone's skills are utilized where they are most capable. When everyone is valued, the result is greater effort by everyone and ending in more success for the group.

Usually this process is accomplished by creating teams in school, church or the workplace. This team method was practiced successfully in the Old Testament by Nehemiah in rebuilding the walls of Jerusalem Nehemiah 4:6: *"So we rebuilt the wall till all of it reached half its height, for the people worked with all their heart."* You can grasp their enthusiastic team spirit. Later they finished the wall, Nehemiah 6:15: *"So the wall was completed on the twenty-fifth of Elul, in fifty-two days."* Later in the New Testament, Jesus used cooperation among the 12 disciples to change the world forever for God's purpose for His people.

Cooperation has been proven with countless studies to be more successful in achieving goals faster and with better quality. Professor Perry W. Buffington, PhD. of the University of Georgia in his article on "Competition versus Cooperation" dated January 2014 states: "If in fact competition brings out the 'beast' in us, then research demonstrates that cooperation surely brings out the 'best' in us. This finding has been held in virtually every occupation, skill, or behavior tested." Later he states: "And not surprisingly, cooperation increases creativity. Unfortunately, most people are not taught cooperative skills." Dr. Scott G. Isaksen, Director for Studies in Creativity, at Buffalo State College, Buffalo, NY states: ". . . attempting to do well and trying to beat others is two separate mental processes. It is impossible to concentrate on both. Of the two, cooperating with yourself and others create a positive outcome and has more rewards." Consequently we see some of the many benefits of cooperation.

To develop cooperation in your family or group, try the following:

Act cooperatively with others. A cooperative act speaks volumes to another person and will encourage them to work cooperatively with you. Often such a kindness leads the receiver to want to pass a similar act on to someone else. Such action reflects the caring one has in their heart. Cooperation demonstrates a Christ-like quality as declared in Psalm 133:1: *"How good and pleasant it is when brothers live together in unity!"* It reduces competition because your focus is on the desire and need to work with that other person versus against them.

Sharing information and ideas. Giving and sharing information and ideas with others increases the possibility that they will work together with you on a mutual project. Demonstrating a sharing attitude with others reflects that you care for them. Such actions are more powerful than a leader telling you about cooperation. This action often leads to others passing along the information to others, creating a ripple effect that helps many. When we share we feel a joy in our hearts, which is what Christ wants from us.

Emphasize using teams. Using teams to lead groups has been very effective in meeting the demands of leadership. Within the church and business, use of leadership teams has been most effective in bringing new ideas and maintaining continuity. Rewards and success are shared with every team member resulting in everyone feeling more valued. When one team member starts to fail, often another more capable team member voluntarily works with the struggling one to improve his/her performance. Teams develop a deep bond of togetherness, which is why individual members in military teams are willing to sacrifice their lives for their fellow teammate. As the old adage goes: "There is no I in team," so competitiveness is reduced.

Practice reciprocity. When someone helps you out of a challenge, you usually want to help them out when they encounter a trial in their lives. This action builds mutual care for each other as opposed to competition where the desire is to undermine your peer. Recently at a Starbuck's drive thru in California someone started paying for their coffee and for the person behind them. The practice is called "paying forward" and this went on that day for 455 people until someone stopped it. This reciprocity event made the national news with many people extolling the kindness demonstrated.

Practicing reciprocity is set forth in 2 Corinthians 9:6: "*Remember this: Whoever sows sparingly will also reap sparingly, and whoever sows generously will also reap generously.*" Thus, you will not only feel a joy when practicing reciprocity, but you will be rewarded for it.

Provide sufficient time. Our lives become so filled with activities that we fail to reserve the necessary time to be cooperative with another person. This fast-paced lifestyle at home and workplace demands quick decisions and actions. Too often we get caught up in that rapid response habit causing us to make bad decisions. By having patience with the cooperation process, we make better decisions and take wiser actions. Cooperation requires sufficient time to work out differences and to come to a mutual agreement.

Health benefits. Surveys by researchers have shown that cooperation among workers and members promotes better emotional health than competition. Once you have worked in a cooperative environment, you enjoy more positive feelings about yourself and your compatriots. There is less strife than the "dog eat dog" atmosphere of competition and a feeling of healthy feeling of camaraderie sweeps through the group. In fact, *USA Today*, June, 13 2014 discussed a study from "Too much arguing is bad for your health." The study goes on to stress that: ". . . people who worry about partners and children or perceive that those family members 'demand too much' face a higher risk of early death."

One of the dangers of cooperation is "group think" where everyone becomes a "yes" person to everything that the leaders propose. Such group thinking can easily lead to disastrous results. Witness the corporate culture at GM having to recall over 18 million cars to fix a simple problem that many employees knew about for over 10 years. We need to be responsible by facing issues head on, dealing with them, and not living in denial. Some additional concepts that minimize intentional favoritism are:

The power of forgiveness. When we have been wounded by favoritism, we expect the offending person to apologize to us for their hurtful action. In the majority of times, this will not occur as the initiator remains unaware or uncaring of their action on us and just goes on with their life. We, on the other hand, very often continue to feel the pain of their original rejection of us as the unfavored one, or their indifference as the overlooked one into our adult lives. Forgiving them is God's answer to releasing us from our prison of pain called bitterness as Jesus states in Luke 6:37: ". . . *forgive and you will be forgiven.*"

If the initiating person never becomes convicted of their sin, our expectations for an apology from him/her will never be realized. Nevertheless, we have the option of exercising one-sided forgiveness, whereby we forgive the person that brought the favoritism into our lives. We do this knowing that the other person may never ask for forgiveness. Through forgiveness, we discover a new freedom in our hearts.

Listen to understand the other person. To truly understanding someone's message requires you to listen closely to their words plus discern their emotions behind the words. Our words have power so when we use careless words they can hurt others. Proverbs 12:18: *"Reckless words pierce like a sword, but the tongue of the wise brings healing."* Also, we are often unclear when expressing our feelings and ideas. Consequently, our message becomes confusing and frustrating resulting in misunderstandings. When our words and the emotions reflect a different message, the emotions probably reveal the true message.

Leon, an African-American student at Syracuse Teen Challenge with a heart for helping others, started working with two other new African-American students. He realized that these recent arrivals lacked an understanding of Christianity and the Bible. Patiently, he listened to their many questions and gave them solid biblical answers. Leon also spent his free time helping them to find godly answers for their various doubts about Christianity. Over time, his effort helped several students to understand the deep truths of the Bible.

Yet, all people yearn to be understood. Some suggestions to improve communication are:

Reflective listening. This process is using many of the same words of the other person when replying to them. In effect, you are like a mirror reflecting their words back to them to make sure you understand them. They feel more connected with your reply when you use their own words and mutual understanding improves. Example: "This is what I heard you say . . . . . . " Careful listening reflects Christian love to the other person, which is the opposite of partiality.

Asking questions is less confrontational. When you use questions versus statements, your comments are less judgmental of the other person. You appear to be collecting information as opposed to judging them. People often become defensive and stop talking or lash back at any hint of correction. As a result, using questions allows you to proceed with your message in a different form thereby enlightening understanding.

Being empathetic. Empathy is defined by *Webster's* as: "the capacity for participating in or a vicarious experiencing of another's feeling, violations, or ideas . . ." Being empathetic to another's pain or situation enables you to connect with their emotional state. They may exclaim: "You really do understand me and my condition!" Thus they will want to receive your message and mutual understanding grows. Empathy counters the attitude of "it's all about me" characteristic of favoritism.

Giving to others. When we give of our money, time, and effort to others we diminish our inborn self-centeredness, which is a prime characteristic of favoritism. We are born focusing on our own needs. Later we learn from Christian principles and the importance of giving to others. Jesus commands us in Luke 6:38: *"'Give and it will be given to you. A good measure, pressed down, shaken together and running over, will be poured into your lap. For with the measure you use, it will be measured to you.'"* Thus giving is an act of love and kindness, which are major Christian principles.

Giving helps us overcome selfish greed, which is a part of favoritism. When our focus is on accumulating material possessions and money, this effort can cause us to view them as our god instead of the real God. Such action is a sin. Therefore, giving helps us change our focus from our needs to those of others. The apostle John addresses this point in 1 John 3:17-18: *"If anyone has material possessions and sees his brother in need but has no pity on him, how can the love of God be in him? Dear children, let us not love with words or tongue but with actions and in truth."* Also, we are more humbled when we give.

If we utilize these above principles, they will reduce and help to heal the anguish of intentional favoritism that afflicts too many of us. Reducing this partiality in everyone's lives will improve the emotional and spiritual health of us all—favorite one, unfavored one, and overlooked one.

Summary:

1. Favoritism is a fact in every family or group as it impersonates love. When favoritism is intentional, it is destructive to everyone.

2. Intentional favoritism develops when the authority uses it to get a member to get the authority's goals. It doesn't always benefit the favorite. Favoritism hurts us by:

a. Impairs our relationship with Jesus. Our relationship with Jesus is our main source of strength and direction. John 15 5-6. Striving to be the favorite distracts us from this relationship. Putting worldly goals ahead of Christ violates the first commandment, Exodus 20:3.

b. Ruptures your relationships with family or friends. When a family member is constantly praised and rewarded by our mutual authority, we feel angry. We usually blame the favored family member instead of the authority who started it.

c. Brings a sense of entitlement. The more attention we receive the more we want and expect it constantly from the authority. We treat unfavored ones as less than ourselves and become very prideful.

d. Breaks boundaries purposely. Favorites feel that they are above the rules so they purposely break them, expecting no discipline. They will eventually destroy themselves. Proverbs 16:18.

e. Everyone seeks to become a favorite. Favorites get the major rewards so everyone seeks to become a "favorite" and so defeating others becomes a goal. They use evil tactics to win. Favoritism breaks down team cooperation resulting in team goals not being reached—everyone loses and the organization fails.

f. People become self-centered. Favorites usually get whatever they desire causing them to want more. They get a fleeting not lasting satisfaction. They miss the enduring fulfillment of knowing Jesus, family and friends. Ecclesiastes 2:1 and 13. To minimize the affect of intentional favoritism, use the following suggestions:

a. Using cooperation versus competition in groups. Our society believes strongly in the value of competition to select favorites. Competition starts with parents having their children vie for attention and continues in school then work. It thrives in churches as members vie for power positions. Competition creates a few winners, but many more resentful losers. Their ideas and work are not appreciated so they become apathetic in: attendance, work, and quality of work. Often they leave in silent protest.

b. Cooperation is parties working together to achieve a common goal. Everyone's ideas are welcomed and they feel a part of the group. 1 Corinthians 12:14. Everyone's skills are used creating group success. It is accomplished by creating teams in school, church or workplace. Nehemiah 4:6 and 6:15. Jesus used cooperation to accomplish great things. In many studies, cooperation has proven to be more successful than competition in achieving goals faster with better quality.

c. To develop cooperation and reduce competition use the following:

1). Act cooperatively with others. A cooperative act to another person encourages them to work with you. Often the receiver will pass along a similar act to someone else—a Christlike quality. Psalm 133:1.

2). Sharing information and ideas. Sharing ideas with others encourages them to work with you and shows a caring attitude. It leads to others to also pass along the idea to others, helping many.

3). Emphasize using teams to lead groups not single individuals. They are most effective in developing new ideas and maintaining continuity. Rewards and success are shared, as each member feels valued. Members develop a deep bond.

4). Practice reciprocity. Help someone with a challenge and they will help you out of your trial, thereby building mutual care. 2 Corinthians 9:6.

5). Provide sufficient time. Cooperation requires time to communicate with another person. Often we react resulting in bad decisions versus the cooperative response ending in wiser decisions.

6). Health benefits. Surveys show that cooperation promotes better emotional health. A cooperative environment promotes positive feelings about yourself and others with less strife.

d. A danger of cooperation is "group think," when everyone approves everything that the leaders propose can lead to disaster. We need to responsibly face issues.

Some further concepts that minimize intentional favoritism are:

1. Listen to understand the other person. Listening to their words plus the emotions behind the words leads to understanding. Words have power that can hurt others. Proverbs 12:18. We are unclear in expressing our feelings and ideas, which creates misunderstandings. Some suggestions to improve communication are:

a. Reflective listening. By using the words of the other person when replying to them, they feel more connected with your reply which improves understanding.

b. Ask questions. Use questions instead of statements as they are less judgmental. Questions imply seeking information and not correction, which helps communication.

c. Being empathetic. Empathy is defined as: "the capacity for participating in or a vicarious experiencing of another's feeling, violations, or ideas ..." It enables you to connect with their emotional state.

2. Giving to others. Giving money, time, and effort to others reduces our selfishness. It follows the Christian principles in Luke 6:38. It helps us overcome greed and changes our focus from accumulating possessions and money. 1 John 3: 17-18.

Discussion Questions

1. Name three negative characteristics of intentional favoritism?

   Do these features make you never want to use intentional favoritism?

2. If you have ever worked cooperatively with others? What was your experience?

   What were the positive aspects of cooperation that you noticed?

   What negative features occurred?

   Did you encounter "group think?"

3. Would you use cooperation with a group, if you had the opportunity?

   If not, why not?

4. Have you ever used reflective listening? Can you discern another's emotions?

5. When you give to others in some way, what does that do for your life?

Chapter 12
Understanding and Finding God's Favor

We read in the Bible and hear how God gives favor to certain people. Does that imply that God's favor is really intentional favoritism? No. God, in His providence, gives kindness, grants prayer requests and bestows His blessings generously, but not always in a material manner. He did, nevertheless, materially bless: Job, Abraham, Joseph, David and Solomon. It is important to note, however, that those He did show material favor to had to endure great suffering and/or trials. Such an example is Job who suffered greatly when all his possessions as well as his children were taken from him in one day, not to mention his subsequent physical afflictions.

Later, God restored all his material losses and blessed him with new children. God does show favor to those who are chosen to carry out His plan. As I have noted in several previous chapters of this book, the authority, using intentional favoritism, usually excuses the favored one from most discipline and protects them from experiencing most trials. Consequently, receiving God's favor is definitely not the same as intentional favoritism.

When we, in faith, ask God for forgiveness of our sins and accept Jesus as the Lord and leader of our lives, God grants us His grace of forgiveness of our sins and eternal life. We then become saved followers of Christ and thereby receive His favor as long as we don't endanger that through continuous grievous sin. Unfortunately, God's grace has been marginalized by a group in the church, The Grace Movement, which waters down the cost of grace by treating it as a "get out of jail" card. It is the "once saved always saved" message that neglects God's admonition to refrain from continuing to sin and to be holy and righteous throughout our life. Titus 2:12 commands us: ". . . *to deny ungodliness and worldly desires and to live sensibly, righteously, and godly in the present age."*

Dietrich Bonhoeffer, the great German theologian, attacked such theology as "cheap grace" in his book, *The Cost of Discipleship,* declaring: "Cheap grace is the preaching of forgiveness without requiring repentance, (it is) baptism without church discipline, Communion without confession, absolution without personal confession. Cheap grace is grace without discipleship, grace without the cross, grace without Jesus Christ, living and incarnate." Instead, Bonhoeffer, in the same book, calls all Christ followers to recognize the actual cost of grace: "Such grace is *costly* because it calls us to follow, and it is *grace* because it calls us to follow *Jesus Christ*. It is costly because it costs a man his life, and it is grace because it gives a man the only true life. It is costly because it condemns sin, and grace because it justifies the sinner. Above all, it is costly because it cost God the life of his Son: 'ye were bought at a price,' and what has cost God much cannot be cheap for us."

In the Bible, God blessed many of His followers with His favor. Some notable examples are: Noah, Esther, Daniel, Mary the mother of Jesus, and, of course, Jesus. So what is God's favor and how can I be blessed myself? Many biblical scholars believe that God, in His sovereignty, blesses certain followers with His favor, or approval while also giving them certain qualities like leadership or prophesy to accomplish His plan through them. For example, God gave Joseph the ability to interpret dreams, which later led to the saving of the Jewish nation from famine. The Bible reveals some of the qualities of the person who receives God's favor are:

> **Dedicated believers** whose hearts are turned toward God. They believe deeply in the Lord and trust Him so totally that they are willing to give up their very lives for Him. Their hearts are totally committed to Him. A good example is David when he was first anointed as king of Israel as stated in 1 Samuel 16:7: "*. . . Man looks at the outward appearance, but the Lord looks at the heart.*" The Lord considered David a man of His own heart so He also is look-

ing into your heart. What will He find?

Devoted followers who daily worship and pray to the Lord. They have a genuine, abiding friendship with the Lord that results in them wanting to follow His commandments and admonitions, even when threatened with danger. Their wills are faithful to following the Lord's commandments out of this close relationship. When they commit a sin they know it hurts that relationship and are convicted to quickly ask God for forgiveness. A strong example is Daniel who was threatened for daily praying to God, but he did so anyway knowing he was breaking the law. For that he faced the lions den (Daniel 6:6-21). Proverbs 3:1: *"My son do not forget my teaching, but keep my commands in your heart."* Are you willing to follow His commandments with all your will, despite any danger or rejection?

Dependent on God's wisdom for their lives. Proverbs 8:35: *"For whoever finds me* (wisdom) *finds life and receives the favor from the Lord."* They submitted to God's wisdom regularly to guide them into making wise choices and decisions, which directed their walk toward His plan for their lives. A biblical example would be Samuel who started living with the priests at about two years of age and sought God's direction throughout his life (1 Samuel 1:24-16:13). Are you willing to submit to following God's directions for all your decisions and actions?

> When I was in my 29th year at the bank, I received an early retirement offer in the Spring of that year. If I accepted it, I would have been retired later that same year. I was very surprised since I was only 56 years old at the time and felt I had several more years before I really wanted to retire. So I felt, using my human wisdom, that this was not the right move for me. Nevertheless, I decided to discuss the offer with a wise Christian friend and ask his

advice. He suggested that I throw out a fleece to determine God's will in my situation, like Gideon did in Judges 6:36-40. My fleece was purposely turning in my application one day beyond the deadline as a test of God's will for this decision. If the bank accepted it, I would see that as a sign of God's will to take the early retirement.

At the same time, I started praying daily to God for His direction for this important decision, since I had felt called to follow Him. Within a month, the bank accepted my application, so now I had the option to accept it or not. My decision was to trust God with my future or stay at the bank and save more funds for retirement. I felt called by my faith and trust in the Lord to accept the retirement offer. As a result, the decision makers at the head office in New York City decided to close my regional office, which caused me to feel sad for my fellow employees who now had to find new jobs. Later, my boss told me that they were looking to close my office next year anyway and move me back to New York City from Syracuse. I marveled how God was aware of this and had guided me once I trusted Him with this enormous decision.

Since then I have volunteered at the Syracuse Rescue Mission and Syracuse Teen Challenge. At both places, I found greater peace in my life as God introduced me to working with people in poverty and drug addicts. He also opened up a ministry for me in teaching and writing on such topics as anger, conflict, bitterness, and favoritism. To see God set people free from the anguish of such things brings me joy I never would have known had I stayed at the bank. God's plans are, indeed, far better than anything I could have imagined.

Determined when going through trials, rejection, and judgment by others. For example: Mary, the mother of Jesus, had to endure the public shame of being an unwed pregnant teenager; King David lost three of his sons to premature deaths; and Noah probably suffered the public ridicule for building an ark during a long drought. Yet, they all persevered through their trials in following God. Revelation 3:10: *"Since you have kept my command to endure patiently, I will also keep you from the hour of trial that is going to come upon the whole world to test those who live on the earth."*

This process was sometimes used as part of God's cleansing of His followers of their ungodly attitudes. Some examples: Joseph was unjustly jailed for over two up to possibly 13 years to humble him and remove the conceit from his life. Paul (first called Saul) initially hated and killed Christians, but was chosen by God through a dramatic confrontation with Jesus. Yet, he had to go through three years of further refining before being released into his ministry for Christ. Acts 9:3-6: *"As he neared Damascus on his journey, suddenly a light from heaven flashed around him. He fell to the ground and heard a voice say to him, 'Saul, Saul, why do you persecute me? Who are you Lord?' Saul asked. 'I am Jesus, whom you are persecuting,' he replied. 'Now get up and go into the city, and you will be told what you must do.'"* Psalm 66:10 speaks to God's refining process: *"For you, O God, tested us; you refined us like silver."* Are you willing to let God to refine you with trials, or suffering for His greater purpose?

Daring to surrender their future plans for God's destiny. This action often required them to make drastic changes in their lives and occupations. A prime example was Moses, originally a prince in Egypt, who left all his worldly luxury behind to be ultimately exalted by God to lead the nation of Israel out of bondage into the promised land. Hebrews 11:24-26 relays how Moses through faith gave up his royal future for God's plan: *"By faith when Moses had grown up, refused to be known as the son of Pharaoh's daughter. He chose to be for a mistreated along with the people of God rather than to enjoy the pleasures of sin short time. He regarded disgrace for the sake of Christ as of greater value than the* *treasures of Egypt, because he was looking ahead to his reward."*

Some of God's followers exhibited these above qualities, yet they did not receive God's favor because of their ungodly expectations like wanting greater wealth, but also their negative attitudes about others like the Pharisees in the New Testament. Thus, God's favor is not based entirely on our performance. It is still God's sovereign decision as to who he will favor and who He will not. God wants to show His favor to each one of us as we follow Him daily. He blessed Jehoahaz as found in 2 Kings 13:4: *"Then Jehoahaz sought the Lord's favor, and the Lord listened to him . . . ."* Unfortunately, too often we reject His attempts to favor us because we really want our own plan or we don't understand that His plan is the best for our future. Are you willing to give up your expectations for God's better plan?

The benefits that may come to us if we are blessed by God's favor are:

Protection from danger, Satan, and our enemies. His supreme protection helps us to overcome our fears and allows us to walk through danger(s) leaning on our faith in Christ. Psalm 5:12: *"For surely you bless the righteous; you surround them with your favor as with a shield."*

A new confidence and strength to carry out His purpose through us. We feel a renewed assurance in our minds that we can achieve great accomplishments for Christ. Philippians 1:6: *"being confident of this, that he who began a good work in you, will carry it on to completion until the day of Christ Jesus."*

Spiritual blessings. We are given a closer and deeper relationship with Christ. We sense His walking with us throughout the day and He is there to help us through our challenges. Ephesians 1:3: *"Praise be to the God and Father of our Lord Jesus Christ, who has blessed us in the heavenly realms with every spiritual blessing in Christ."* Some examples of these spiritual blessings as listed in Ephesians

1:4-12 are: assurance of eternal salvation, adoption as His children, no condemnation, and the forgiveness of our sins through the blood sacrifice of Jesus Christ on the cross as Romans 4:7 reveals: *"Blessed are they whose transgressions are forgiven, whose sins are covered."* He also gives us wisdom and insight to make godly decisions. All these blessings have an eternal value to us and to those who commit to Him.

Answers prayers and requests. God wants to answer our godly prayers, however, in His perfect time. In our human impatience, we often want our prayers answered as soon as possible. That may work against God's greater plan, which we do not know. Esther 7:3: *"Then Queen Esther answered, 'If I have found favor with you, O king, and if it pleases your majesty grant me my life—this is my petition. And spare my people—this is my request.'"*

Peace that passes all understanding from the strife in the world. We all seek this type of all encompassing peace that abides with us through the trials and joys of life. 2 Thessalonians 3:16 declares: *"Now may the Lord of peace himself give you peace at all times and in every way. The Lord be with all of you."*

God wants to bless you with His favor as His follower as stated in Proverbs 12:2: *"Good people obtain favor from the LORD, but he condemns those who devise wicked schemes."* All supporters of God desire His favor as he did for young Samuel in 1 Samuel 2:26: *"And the boy Samuel continued to grow in stature and in favor with the Lord and with men."* He is seeking those of us who commit their hearts and lives to Him as spelled out in 2 Chronicles 16:9: *"For the eyes of the LORD range throughout the earth to strengthen those whose hearts are fully committed to him."* If you take on the characteristics listed above, including the trials and suffering, and follow His plan (costly grace) you will be blessed with His favor.

Summary:

1. In the Bible, God blessed many of His followers with His favor. God blesses some followers with His favor while giving them special qualities to accomplish His plan. Joseph.

2. It is through grace we are saved and given eternal salvation. Bonhoeffer tells us to avoid cheap grace and seek costly grace for our lives.

3. The qualities of the person who receives God's favor are:

a. Dedicated believers whose heart is turned to God. 1 Samuel 16:7. David.

b. Devoted followers who daily worship and pray to the Lord. They want to follow His commandments and admonitions, despite danger. Proverbs 3:1. Daniel.

c. Dependent on God's wisdom in making wise decisions. Proverbs 8:35. Samuel.

d. Determined when going through trials, rejection, and judgment by others to follow God. Paul Acts 9:3-6. They were refined of worldly attitudes. Psalm 66:10. Joseph and Paul.

e. Daring to surrender their future plans for God's destiny for them. It required them to make changes in their lives. Hebrews 11:24-26. Moses.

4. Some followers demonstrate these qualities, but don't receive God's favor as it was not His plan, or their negative attitude. God's favor is not based on performance as He decides who will receive favor. God wants to show favor to all of His followers.

The benefits of God's favor are:

a. God protects us from danger, Satan and our enemies. Psalm 5:2.

b. He gives us a new confidence and strength to carry out His purpose through us. Philippians 1:6.

c. He blesses us in a spiritual way. Ephesians 1:3.

d. Our prayers and requests are more likely to be granted. Esther 7:3.

e. He brings a special peace into our life from the strife of the world. 2 Thessalonians 3:16.

4. God wants to bless us with His favor like young Samuel. 1 Samuel 2:26. He wants those who commit their lives to Him to recognize that enduring trials may be a part of His plan.

Discussion Questions

1. Name three of the characteristics of those that are favored.

   Do you think that today you would qualify for God's favor?

   If not, why not?

2. Explain the difference between "cheap grace" and "costly grace."

3. Name the benefits. Which one appeals to you?

4. Have you ever felt that God blessed you with His favor?

   If so, in what areas were you blessed?

   Are you willing to go through the suffering God may give you to get His favor?

Epilogue

I specifically chose the word anguish in my title to characterize favoritism. *Webster's Dictionary* defines anguish as: "extreme pain of body or mind: excruciating distress." So why is favoritism so painful to us when so much of it occurs regularly over our lives? My research shows that too many times a simple preference morphs into intentional favoritism by an authority. What initially seems benign ends up severely harming the lives of everyone involved—the favored one, unfavored one, the overlooked one, and even the misguided authority. Each one of us is in one of these states now and may encounter all four at different times in our lives.

Initially the pain of exclusion from love and affirmation is felt first by the unfavored one. They feel unfairly rejected for no valid reason by the authority. Ironically, while they recognize the unfairness of their situation, they still mistakenly try to get some morsel of approval. When that too is rejected, the unfavored one falls into a deepening resentment or despair over their situation. They think, "Am I worthy of any love?" They grope to find answers and without God helping and directing them, they can sink into a deep depression.

Meanwhile, the overlooked one strives for attention of some kind and may even seek negative attention, which they prefer to no attention at all. Those overlooked ones usually grasp their true situation quicker than the unfavored ones and seek help outside the family, usually with friends. Depending on the maturity and wisdom of their friends they can be led into very negative situations like drugs or gangs. They, too, question whether they are loveable. Again, seeking God provides the real help for them.

The favorite seems to get everything and initially they are happy.

However, that fleeting happiness is lost as they aspire for more rewards without working for them. Their prideful attitude becomes their downfall as they eventually lose personal relationships and even their achievements. Finally, the misguided authority who's intentional favoritism initially started this destruction discovers his intentional favoritism can leave him/her isolated and resented by their unfavored and overlooked children or members. Their favorite, meanwhile, may even pull away from them leaving the authority alone.

Consequently, we all can become losers to intentional favoritism. In the end, it is a deception by Satan to destroy families, churches and businesses. First, all of us needs to realize when it is happening and then take action to reduce its affects. Next each party needs to seek spiritual help from God in prayer and strength from His Word. Then, find help from an older mature Christian adult who can listen and guide you. Favorites recognizing their unfair position should give it up, or ask their authority to give some of their rewards and affirmation to the unfavored and overlooked ones. Through group pressure from family or members, we can point out the many dangers of intentional favoritism to the authority by asking them to stop it.

It is my hope that readers using the suggestions in this book will be able to effectively reduce any intentional favoritism in their lives and of those around them. This book can be used effectively in small groups to help more people hurting from the damage of intentional favoritism. By drawing close to the source of true love, Jesus Christ, everyone will be able to avoid the counterfeit love of intentional favoritism and find a new sense of freedom.

I welcome your feedback and questions from this book. If you enjoyed this book, you might find one or more of my other books of interest to you.

Anger Reconciliation
It discusses anger with a biblical, effective way to express it.

Anger Reconciliation Workbook
It follows the book, but could be used individually.

From Bitterness to Reconciliation
Anger held in becomes bitterness. The book provides a reader with steps for healing through intentional forgiveness.

From Bitterness to Reconciliation Workbook
It follows the book, but may be used separately.

James Offutt
Email: offutt2@hotmail.com
Telephone: 315-395-4310

Notes

Chapter 1
What is Favoritism?

1. Ellen Webber Libby PhD., *The Favorite Child* (Amherst, NY, Prometheus Books 2010) p.19.

2. Bonnie Angelos, *First Mothers: The Women Who Shaped the Presidents* (New York, Harper, 2006).

3. Libby, *The Favorite* p. 20-21.

Chapter 2
How Favoritism Originates In the Home, Church, and Workplace

Chapter 3
The Favored One: The Advantages & Disadvantages

1. Libby, *The Favorite*. p. 69.

Chapter 4
The Unfavored One & The Overlooked One:
The Advantages & Disadvantages

1. Libby, *The Favorite* p. 255.

2. Ibid. p. 47.

3. Karl Pillemer, Jill Suitor, Seth Pardo, Charles Henderson, article *Mothers' Differentiation and Depressive Symptoms among Adult Children, Journal of Marriage and Family.* published by The National Council of Family Relations, Minneapolis, Minn. April 10, 2010.

4. Jeffrey Kluger, *The Sibling Affect*, Riverhead Books, NY, 2011, p. 97.

5. Ibid. p.95.

6. Catherine Salmon, *The Secret Power of Middle Children: How Middleborns Can Harness Their Unexpected and Remarkable Abilities*, Hudson Press, p. 55.

7. Ibid. p.74.

Chapter 5
Destructive Pride: A Major Element of the Favorite

1. Dr. Les Carter and Dr. Frank Minirth, *Anger Workbook,* Thomas Nelson, Inc, Nashville, Tennessee, 1993, p.119.

2. C.J. Mahaney and Joshua Harris, *Humility: True Greatness,* Multnomah Publishers Inc. Sisters, Oregon, 2005, p.31.

3. Dr. Les Carter, *The Anger Trap,* Jossey-Bass. A Wiley Imprint, San Francisco, CA, 2003, p.88.

4. Les Carter and Dr. Frank Minirth, *Anger,* p.120.

5. Dr. Les Carter, *The Anger,* p.92.

6. C.J. Mahaney and Joshua Harris, *Humility,* p. 20.

Chapter 6
Favoritism From Childhood to Teenage Years

1. Linda Sonna PhD, *The Everything Parent's Guide To Raising Siblings,* F+W Publications,Inc.2006, p.128.

2. Study by Catherine Conger, *Time Magazine,* article "Playing Favorites" by Jeffery Kluger, Oct. 3, 2011. p. 2.

3. Carol Kuykendall, *Five-Star Families,* Fleming Revel a division of Baker Publishing, Grand rapids, MI, 2005, p. 60-64.

4. Linda Sonna Phd, *The Everything.* p. 34.

Chapter 7
Favoritism: Teenage Years into Adult Years

1. Linda Sonna Phd, *The Everything.* p. 49.

2. Carol Kuykendall, *Five-Star.* p. 120.

3. Jane Isay, *Mom Likes You Best,* Doubleday a division of Random House, New York, NY, 2010, p.53-54.

4. Karl Pillemer, Jill Suitor "Journal of Marriage."

5. Jeanne Safer, *Cain's Legacy,* Basic Books a member of the Perseus Books Group, New York, NY, 2012, p. 2.

Chapter 8
Favoritism in the Bible

1. Jeanne Safer, *Cain's Legacy,* p. 20-21.

2. Henry M. Morris, *The Genesis Record: A scientific & devotional commentary on the book of beginnings,* Bakerbooks a division of Baker Publishing, Grand rapids, MI, p. 52.

3. Matthew Henry, *Matthew Henry's Commentary on the Bible.*

4. Jeanne Safer, *Cain's Legacy,* p. 44.

Chapter 9
Favoritism in Church

Chapter 10
Favoritism in the Workplace

1. A study issued by Georgetown University McDonough School of Business, Georgetown, MD, issued August 23, 2011. It was conducted by the research firm of Penn Schoen Berland, which surveyed 303 senior business executives of companies of at least 1,000 employees.

Chapter 11
How to Reduce Favoritism in Our Lives

1. Dr. Les Carter, *The Anger,* p. 88.

2. Professor Perry W. Buffington, PhD. of the University of Georgia, article on "Competition vs Cooperation," Goodwill, January 2014.

3. *USA Today,* article titled "To Live Longer Fight Less," June, 13 2014.

Chapter 12
Understanding and Finding God's Favor

1. Dietrich Bonhoeffer, *Cost of Discipleship,* (MacMillan Company, NY, NY 1949) p. 44.

2. Ibid. p. 45.